T0171464

SOMEONE'S
FOUND A FRIEND

A Documentation of the Wonderful
Spritual Journey of

GRACE NIGHTINGALE

BALBOA.
PRESS

A DIVISION OF HAY HOUSE

ISBN: 978-1-4525-6100-4 (hc)
ISBN: 978-1-4525-6101-1 (e)

Balboa Press books may be ordered through booksellers or by contacting:

Balboa Press
A Division of Hay House
1663 Liberty Drive
Bloomington, IN 47403
www.balboapress.com
1-(877) 407-4847

Images © Grace Nightingale 2012

Printed in the United States of America

Balboa Press rev. date: 12/05/2012

I would like to dedicate this book to my teachers, firstly my father who taught me not to expect anything from anyone, to Pat, Niclaire, Beverly and Sheryle for their love, care and guidance. A special thank you to Margaret Cousins for her patience, guidance and belief in me, for as you will see, without her this book wouldn't exist. Last but not least, I thank my Spirit Guides for their unconditional love and devotion.

I would like to give my sincerest thanks to Penny who made the original suggestion of writing a book to illustrate my journey; to Douglas for his guidance by gently nudging me in the right direction along my path! Yes I had noticed!! Also to say a heart warming thank you to Tacker, Wendy and Pauline for their support, humour and sheer hard work in helping me to get this chronicle into a form that would be enjoyed and understood by many.

Am I a white witch?
Am I a medium?
Am I a healer?
Or a village wise woman?

I don't know, but come with me on my journey to find out.

Contents

Introduction . . . . *xv*

Our first meeting with Margaret. *1*

Our first Meditation *2*

Ball Cleansing Meditation *12*

Ball Cleansing Meditation with Tom *15*

A heart Chakra healing and a Meditation with Margaret *18*

A Little Reflection *28*

My own Meditation *30*

Margaret's Advice *33*

A short Meditation at Home *35*

Crystals *37*

The Room *43*

A Meditation like no other *48*

Just Margaret and Me *55*

Working with Marie-Anne *60*

Some of the Best Love *66*

The Indian Village *70*

Just Wow! *77*

Presents *85*

A Trip to Maiden Castle *90*

A Christmas Visit *99*

Our Visit to Badbury Rings *104*

Sorting Out the Fakes *108*

Ying and Yang *111*

Angel Wings! *114*

The Tunnel of Light *116*

Which Pathway? 123

A Plan for the Future 127

Bill 130

Have Another Go! .133

Which Flight? 139

A Bit of a telling Off 143

The Dream 148

A Test 151

A Calming of my Mind 156

The Pyramid 159

The Inheritance 162

Celestial Hands 166

The Theatre 171

Teamwork 180

Obstacles 183

Truly Remarkable Gifts 189

Chamberly Clairvoyance evening with Sheryle Lewindon . . .194

Healing with Margaret's New Guide 197

An Important Lesson 199

Tacker 205

Sharamana 209

Messages and Guides 214

Tacker's Indian village Trip and My Surprise 219

Thailand 222

The Biggest Surprise of All 228

Epilogue 232

To You All, ...234

Glossary 237

Introduction

I lived in the South of England, a little town called Netherminster.

I am one of four children: John is the oldest by a year; then me; followed by two younger sisters, Claire a year younger; Julie four years younger.

Dad was a cockney, born within the sound of Bow Bells, and had a hard upbringing. He worked tirelessly to provide for us. Mum was born in Plymouth and has always been a loving and giving soul who worked hard to make ends meet.

We lived in a rented house owned by the local council, which wasn't posh but felt 'lived-in'. Being a rural little town, the estate wasn't big, but the kind of place where everyone knew everyone else. It was great. I grew up with lots of friends and neighbours who were lovely to know.

I think we had a fairly normal upbringing, nothing out of the ordinary. My brother was dyslexic and used to get picked on a bit. I felt protective towards him, and would bring any aggressor, regardless of their size, to their knees, with the aid of the backlash from a sharp, formidable tongue! I hasten to add I do think I've mellowed since then.

I went to the local comprehensive school and at the age of fourteen my parents got me a Saturday job in the next town. It was at a busy, local, family-run business that had a shop, café, and restaurant.

Never being frightened of hard work, I started a career in catering, washing up and waitressing, and loved it, meeting lots of people, and learning a great deal. Along with the hard work we also had a good laugh.

At the age of sixteen I was offered a post as assistant cook, which I was thrilled with, and did day release to college.

The catering held me in good stead for many things: from feeding what must have been the five thousand over the years, in different jobs, to making some great friends, and learning a trade.

At home I had a lovely neighbour, Philip, whom I class as my second dad. He used to give me a lift into work on the back of his motorbike. He was a huge man whom others were respectful of. To me, he was like a big teddy with a gentle, soft nature. Philip taught me to ride my own motorbike, (Dad said he wouldn't be a taxi, so we had to find our own way!)

I did six miles round Philip's works' yard, wobbling my way round, before he let me out on the road, to eventually ride my motorbike home for the first time.

With hands shaking, knees knocking against the tank, I made it!

Philip followed behind me like a proud, protective swan, looking after one of his offspring. "Don't ride too near to the hedge or the car drivers will push you in," he said, giving me some good advice.

On that day when I arrived home, mum and a reception committee were waiting at the garden gate, waving and cheering to see me come up the road. Philip bless him, must have phoned ahead.

We had many an early start, so that Philip could take me round the town to get me used to the roads and traffic, before he started work. I used to go miles out of my way to avoid a roundabout or a set of traffic lights, and needed some confidence building. One morning, being 'Miss Independent', I decided I would go into work under my own steam. I was the proud owner of a Yamaha FS1E 50 and 'unrestricted' I'll have you know! It would do 60mph downhill with the wind behind you, on a good day, and conked out on the side of the road on the six miles between home and work, on a bad day.

On this particular Saturday morning, to get to work which was six miles away, I could use the back roads which were quiet, and the easy route, or give myself a push to independence. I decided to do the busy route, which included THE roundabout situated at the bottom end of the town, huge, busy and terrifying, followed by a busy set of traffic lights situated at the top of town, by the Guild hall, where everybody could see you.

On the route there was a point of no return, which meant that if I chickened out I could turn off and join the quiet back roads. On the six miles into town I talked myself (not too brilliantly) into the brave route, passing the point of no return.

I was now heading for THE roundabout, my heart racing, counting down the gears (as a real novice you do that!), slowing down trying not to panic, I approached the roundabout and nobody was on it!

Relieved but now sweating, I was heading right up through town to THE traffic lights, and as I did I noticed a group of kids, about the same age as myself, under the town hall clock, beside the lights.

Right about now absolute panic set in!!

What if I stalled it in front of them fell off? Then made myself look a right Charlie?

Oh God! Now I had lost count of the gears, and the lights had gone red! My knees resumed their knocking on the tank, my hands shaking like a nervous wreck. I stopped, pulled in the clutch, kicked my gears, (hopefully to the 1st gear) and slowed to a halt.

Not daring to look to my left for fear of recognition, in case all failed, I stared straight ahead at the lights.

My bike still going, my heart in my throat, the lights changed. I gave it a handful of throttle (to keep the revs up and not stall), dropped the clutch and I was off! The front wheel rose off the ground and I took off to the other end of town on one wheel, for a hundred yards, like the new Hells Angel on the block!

Amid cheers of appreciation from the assembled crowd, and screaming "Oh shit" I somehow managed to bring it to a near halt, and gracefully turned off to the road leading to my works. How I ever kept it upright I'll never know!

I entered the building a little flushed, pumped with adrenalin, with a feeling that it might be a while till I tried that one wheel thing again.

Talking to a friend years later, I heard that I had had quite the reputation as a real girl biker.

In the end, both my sisters Claire and Julie joined me in passing the tests and having bikes: our brother John didn't bother.

Moving on. I was introduced to Thomas, my husband, by a friend at college, and we have been married for twenty-four years, with two sons, Richard, twenty-two and Harry, nineteen.

We had our challenges along the way, as you do being a parent, with tears and laughter and with firm boundaries. We never had much and spent time making things, like cakes, pastry, scones, taking the boys out on bikes and using up the their energy: anything that was not going to cost a lot. Our prized toy was a big bucket of Lego with a bit of mecano mixed in, which used to keep the boys amused for hours, it was worth its weight in gold.

When they were a little older, the boys would disappear into the shed, with a lot of banging and bumping, sawing and mumbling going on. Then the shed door would fly open and some wonderful contraption would appear, just like the A Team! I lost count of the number of things that they made, also the amount of things that disappeared. They would ride the latest contraption round the garden, only for a wheel or something to fall off. In the shed they went again, a bit more bashing and banging, then silence. . . The door would fly open again, and a new and improved version would emerge, the boys with grins on their faces from ear to ear, and shrieks of laughter as they raced round again. When it came to DIY I don't think Tom had many bits of wood or many nails left that he could call his own.

Raising two boys taught me to love in a different way, to give love unconditionally, to love them for who and what they are, and at the same time keep a tight rein on them, so their actions were caring and respectful of others. For me that was the start, I think, to look at life differently. When you have children who look to you for help, love, and guidance, you tend not to think so much of yourself. The ME of my childhood had grown up and I became a more loving, protective, caring mother.

As Richard and Harry were growing up, Tom showed them how to mend things: firstly toys that broke, then bikes, until they had a lucky break with a broken- down motorbike. Tom taught them how to repair it, and then how to ride it. That was the start of a 'bike phase' in our house, where over the years they bought any old broken motorbike, mended it, and sold it on so they could get a better one. They even restored and sold on a really old valuable model, so they could make enough money to improve the bikes they wanted for themselves.

Eventually, it ended up with both boys having bikes, and along with Tom who was realizing a childhood dream, they went racing them. They had great fun.

I started to have interests of my own, wishing to do something different.

To begin with, I'll explain that for as long as I can remember, I have had awareness that I could make people's bumps and bruises feel better, just by thinking about it.

At school, I remember feeling a bump in the air above a friend's arm that had been broken. I didn't try to do anything to it, but I think it was my first experience of 'feeling' a big injury. Another friend made note of my hands, saying, "Grace your hands fascinate me", but she didn't elaborate. The comment stayed with me. I thought that she meant they were funny, because they were short, fat and stumpy, not elegant like everyone else's! I've no idea how this 'knowledge' about feeling bumps and helping them get better, ever came about, it was something I just knew. It was a bit of a joke amongst members of my family, in later years, especially the boys, that any healing I did was classed as 'mum's voodoo!' I could 'feel' when something wasn't right, I couldn't tell you what it was, or why it felt wrong, but it just felt different under my hands. I could help ease, sometimes extinguish pain, by putting my hands on or over the area that was tender. Then by sending love to the area, it always seemed to feel better.

I became interested in complementary therapies, and studied the art of Thai massage, here in England, for three years, and travelled to Thailand as part of the course. Thailand is a beautiful country, and their massage is a treasure, passed down through the generations, forming a big part of their culture. The Thai people are beautiful inside and out, they are brought up to hurt no thing and no body.

The massage uses stretches, pressure points, and many energy lines throughout the body, to help the natural flow of the body's energy to move freely, unhindered, and to aid good health. A combination of different techniques can help with stiffness in movement, circulation, back and neck pain, and also be enjoyed as a relaxing, regular massage, helping to calm down and release tension created by our hectic world. Altogether a lovely philosophy the Thai people have developed.

It was hard work learning everything, but I absolutely loved it and was determined to pass all my exams, there was no question of a 'may be'. I eventually qualified as a Thai Therapy Practitioner RTT in 2006.

I enjoyed this immensely, meeting different people and bringing a little happiness into people's lives by helping them to feel a little better.

After this, I became interested in Reiki, which originates from India. I studied this for three years, gaining my Reiki Masters qualification in 2010.

Again, as with the Thai, the Reiki is working with the energy flow of the body, but this time in a different way.

Reiki works firstly with certain energy points on the body, which are known as chakras. There are seven main ones. Each chakra is responsible for its own part of the body. By placing hands on or over the chakras, pain and discomfort can be felt in the form of vibrations. Such vibrations can be experienced as heat, cold, prickles and sometimes a strong fuzziness. When the body is healthy its natural vibrations hum.

Reiki involves bringing in universal healing energy, and directing it to the body by means of the hands, to the chakras, or elsewhere that it may be needed, throughout the body.

Each person's body has a slightly different vibration, and each person's body has a lovely soft hum when all is well.

Needing to undertake case studies at the beginning, with both therapies, was a learning curve that I enjoyed, and I continue to find the whole process simply fascinating. Working with the Reiki energies I absolutely love. I thought it could enhance the Thai massage, and found it certainly did.

But in the process of achieving this, I still felt in my heart that there was something missing, there was still a hole, and I wasn't contented. Do you know what I mean?

You just keep on searching, but don't really know what you are searching for? I knew I was looking for something but absolutely no idea what.

Then for no apparent reason, the Masonic Hall in the town where I live started to feel like there was something really special about it, and kept popping into my thoughts. Heaven knows why! I began to feel myself being more and more drawn towards it, every time someone mentioned it I had a warm feeling come over me. It felt so good, like a child drawn to a chocolate box.

I happened to stumble across an advert in the local paper for a clairvoyant evening down at the Hall.

I had attended a clairvoyant evening a long time ago there, which was fairly entertaining though nothing out of the ordinary and no one from the Spirit world came through to me. But I was feeling very curious about what this advert, and an evening such as this, might have in store and why it was drawing me to it.

The local Body and Soul Centre supply opportunities to access different courses and alternative therapy information. I heard they also took charge of the evenings that were advertised at the Masonic Hall, so I thought that was a good place to start.

That particular advertised evening had passed but 'the chocolate box' feeling had not gone away, so I decided to pop along and find out more.

At the Body and Soul Centre I looked at the courses on offer to be held at the Masonic hall. These ranged from slimming to fitness, but none seemed to appeal to me, and there was no clairvoyance mentioned, the missing jigsaw piece wasn't to be found here.

I had also started to feel that I was going to meet someone who would be special. Don't ask me why, it was 'just a feeling'. The original clairvoyant evening was still popping into my thoughts, so I enquired at the centre and I was given times and dates that a series of new clairvoyant sessions would be held there, but the event wasn't going to take place for another three months.

Now being impatient, I decided that maybe that wasn't what I was looking for, and left, slightly disappointed.

Over the next week or so, browsing through my local paper with a cuppa, I noticed that the same clairvoyant session was being advertised on a different evening in the next town.

That's it! I thought I'm going to have to check it out! I asked Tom if he would like to accompany me, and to my surprise he said he would.

I was gob smacked! I didn't think he would come in a million years! I was delighted and so we decided then and there we would go.

The evening arrived and Tom finally admitted that he was absolutely petrified. He had been dreading it all day. Walking across the car park, he mentioned that he thought he would probably be the only man there. I reassured him that he'd be ok, and there would probably be other chaps there. (Well, I was hoping and praying there would be!)

On entering the hall I breathed a sigh of relief. The draw ticket seller on the door was a man. I reassured Tom that of course there would be more men to come.....

Inside, I kept looking around for that person I felt I was supposed to meet, who might be a bit special, but nobody really caught my eye, so being 'brave' we shuffled away from the front of the hall, to the back, to sit and …. hide! We found our seats, and then minutes before the start, a gentleman arrived and made his way to sit down on the chair directly in front of Tom. It turned out that he, in fact, was the only other male in the room. I felt I should point out to Tom that there **was,** now, another guy….. I could breathe a sigh of relief.

To be honest, I too was dreading some aspects of the evening. I hoped and prayed I would not be picked out. I was sure it wasn't the clairvoyance I was really here for, but to meet someone, whoever he or she may be.

Then two doors swung open to the side of the hall. A tall lady who looked like she was aged in her late 30-40's, and another lady, entered the room. I didn't really catch much of a glimpse of the second woman, as only the top of her head was in view to me. I'm not a tall woman and so it seemed, neither was she.

They walked to the front of the stage and the tall lady introduced herself as Sheryle Lewindon.

"I'm Spirit taught. I shoot from the hip and I dish the dirt!" she announced.

Oh dear God, I thought!!! I want me mum!!!!

It was highly entertaining. Sheryle brought through a lot of messages for people who were sat in the audience. Towards the end of the evening, she introduced her assistant, Margaret, and suggested that she should 'have a go' as she put it.

Margaret stood up from her chair and all of a sudden, for the first time that evening, I had a bird's eye view of this lady. She was older than I, probably somewhere in her 60's, and instantly I knew that this was the person I was to meet. Her first words were, "Please be gentle with me...I'm only a fledgling!"

I had the most overwhelming feeling of love come over me for this dear lady, and I had only just clapped eyes on her! Margaret proceeded to do her bit for the evening by starting with a lady who was sat a couple of rows in front of us. She had quite a difficult message that came through for her, and then...she picked out... Tom.

"Can I go to the gentleman over there?" she said pointing at him.

The gent sat in front of Tom thought it was him whom Margaret wanted; he raised his hand and said, "Yes".

"No! Not you, I'm sorry. The gentleman behind," Margaret said.

Then it started. Sheryle stepped forward as well, and with a twinkle in her eye, she joined in, reeling off all the naughty things he had done as a child.

"Would it be true to say that you used to take the tops off the milk bottles, drink the cream, and put the lids back on and put the bottles back?... and who was it who blew up an ants nest?! " Sheryle asked.

Sheryle was on a roll and had Tom banged to rights. Apparently, it was Tom's cousin who put a firework in the ants' nest and blew it to smithereens. Everyone in the room was laughing at the antics these boys had got up to as children.

The evening progressed in a jovial manner and they picked up on many things.

"You have two boys," Sheryle stated, then delivered a message about them.

Margaret picked up on Tom's Grandfather, who lived in the flat below them when they were children. He said to her that he was plagued with loud music from Tom. Bless her, she then reeled off all the heavy metal bands that he was apparently telling her, which I must say, did not sound natural coming from this gentle lady's mouth.

I was determined that I was not going to be picked out of the crowd. I was definitely not here for the floorshow. It was certainly a no- go area and I did sense that Margaret and Sheryle may have felt this also.

Tom, bless him, was sat there through all of his worst fears, as cool as a cucumber, and I felt so proud of him, as I had honestly thought he would bolt for the door if they picked him out. I was indeed very impressed.

Sheryle and Margaret were spot on with everything for Tom. These things were not mind blowing or earth shattering things, but things nobody could have possibly guessed about him. They had to have been in touch with someone. It was amazing!

They say time flies when you are enjoying yourself, and before we knew it, the evening was over. Everyone appeared to have left very quickly, but Tom and I were nattering, I was rummaging for my coat and bag under the seat, and a couple of ladies were still at the front of the hall talking to Sheryle.

Margaret was on her own, so Tom and I grabbed the chance to have a chat and to thank her and Sheryle for a lovely evening.

I felt I had to chat to Margaret and was very drawn to her. As we were talking, I found out that she did healing, then all of a sudden it started to dawn on me that this definitely was the person I was looking for.

Margaret reminded me of my old kitchen manager who trained me to her standards, when I was employed within the catering industry. When we worked together there was always great laughter over something or other. (She was a delight to work with, a lovely lady who looked and sounded just like Margaret.)

I felt warmth and affection towards Margaret and I had only just met her. I felt I just wanted to give her a great big hug, and knew in my heart that this was the person I was destined to meet.

Without wanting to scare the woman with a mountain of questions that I was bursting to ask, I enquired as to what exactly it was that she and Sheryle did. When healing was mentioned, I thought that this was my chance to share my interests with her. I explained about the Thai massage and the Reiki I had undertaken, and instantly both Tom and I were invited down to their Centre in Wishdal.

No-one else had received a personal invite that evening, and looking around, there were still a few people wandering around inside and outside the hall, so we felt highly honoured to have been asked.

We decided then and there that we would go down and meet them again.

Over the next few days we researched the centre on the Internet, and found their website. The centre was roughly an hour's drive away, so we thought it a good idea to get in touch before we set off, to make sure they were going to be there, so we e-mailed a message. We didn't get a reply, but we decided to take a chance and go anyway, holding onto the thought that if it was meant to be it would happen, and if not, then maybe this wasn't the path for either of us to follow.

We travelled down by car and reached the Centre where Margaret and Sheryle practiced. Walking in through the door, we met with a wonderful warm welcome. They remembered us both and to be welcomed into their fold was just fantastic. We stayed for the evening, which again involved a clairvoyant evening with Sheryle and Margaret, and this time I didn't mind if I was picked out.

Sheryle picked up on my Grandmother who came through to her with information for me that again, was spot on. But in my mind I kept asking, "Please tell me what I am supposed to do regarding the healing side of things. A signal. Anything. Please. "

Grandmother continued to chatter on about making apple pies, reminiscing about this and that. It all seemed a bit trivial when all of a sudden, Sheryle blurted out that it was about time Tom bought me a bunch of flowers, how he hadn't taken me on holiday for years, and that the number 25 was important. All so true as the following year it would be our 25th wedding anniversary. Nothing was coming through about healing, though. I thanked Sheryle for the messages she had brought through for me, and found it all really fascinating.

At the end of the evening we caught up with Margaret who was free to have a chat. She mentioned that the Centre was going to hold healing courses that may be of interest but which weren't due to start until the January of next year (2009). It was still only July 2008, so my heart sank. Sheryle came over and was talking to me about doing clairvoyance, and I explained I wasn't really that interested in clairvoyance, the idea of standing in front of all those people frightened me silly, and was not for me, it was more the healing aspect I was interested in. With that, she turned to Margaret and told her that she could teach me on a one- to-one basis. Sheryle declared that she had taught Margaret all she knew, and now it was up to Margaret to teach me.

Well, Margaret agreed there and then to tutor us. Yes *us!* Tom *and me*. You could have knocked me down with a feather. I was so, so thrilled. I didn't care if it was going to cost the earth I *had* to do this, it felt so right.

We later found out that the clairvoyance evening we had attended in Wishdal was supposed to have been run by another person who had, unfortunately, fallen ill. Sheryle and Margaret had stepped in at the last minute. So for me… it just about confirmed it… This was meant to be.

The next chapters are accounts of the work that I have undertaken with Margaret. On a personal level, I find it all quite amazing. It's my personal journey, but one that I would like to share with you. I hope you enjoy it, and you never know, it might just be part of your own journey.

Our first meeting with Margaret

ALL THE FOLLOWING EXPERIENCES ARE true and my personal journey. Names and places have been changed to protect the identity of those concerned, except those of my teachers whom wished for their correct names to be used.

After the clairvoyant evening in Wishdal, Margaret invited us down to her house for another evening. I think it was to make sure that we were the sort of people who she would be able to teach, and basically for us all to get to know each other, because after all, bless her heart, she had welcomed us into her home and we were, in fact, total strangers and she didn't know us from Adam.

It was really nice. We chatted all night, and it felt like we had known each other forever. She was so easy to talk to. We arranged a date to start our work together, 17th September 2008.

I didn't really know what we had let ourselves in for, but hoped it might help me to obtain new and different techniques for my healing work

OUR FIRST MEDITATION

17th September 2008

THIS WAS OUR FIRST EVENING as students with Margaret. Tom and I were beside our selves with excitement, and really didn't know what to expect. Margaret had told us we would firstly meet our Spirit Guides and Gatekeepers, and this particular night was for us to meet our Gatekeepers.

This was new to me, and finding out about it all was very interesting. The more I found out, the more I wished to know.

"When you are working with Spirit, your Gatekeeper is responsible for your protection, and has to be aware of everything going on around you.

Everything that *is*, has a vibration.

The Gatekeepers have to know every vibration of the Spiritual level they are on, as well as each one below them. Their training takes a long time, and in some ways, is more difficult than that of your Guides. They do communicate with you, but not as much as your Guides, because they are concentrating on what is around you," Margaret explained.

For as long as I can remember, I had felt the presence of what I thought, was a Roman soldier nearby me, but not knowing anything about all of this, I was intrigued to find out if he was anything to do with our current learning, and couldn't wait to find out more.

Margaret went on, "Now about your Spirit Guides. They are assigned to you to help you throughout this lifetime; they are there if you choose to make contact. You normally have one main Guide, others can come in to join you, and help with different things that are in their field of expertise, depending on what you are doing at a given time in your life. They are there to give you love and to help and Guide you. They may pass their gifts on to you if you are lucky enough and have done whatever is needed to receive them.

Your Guide stands at your right shoulder; your Gatekeeper at your left," Margaret informed.

Apparently, if you do not wish to work with your Guide, they will step back until you wish to make contact. Some people choose not to, that is their choice and *is* fine, but their Guide will always be there waiting for them if they change their mind.

Tom and I had no idea as to where any of this would take us or what we would see or do. It just felt it was the right path to investigate.

So we put ourselves in Margaret's capable hands, and made ourselves comfortable in her front room, Tom sitting on the sofa, me in a warm comfortable chair in the corner. As instructed, our feet were firmly planted on the floor, eyes closed, for the start of an experience of a lifetime!

Margaret explained she would give us instruction and we were to visualise what she was saying.

At the start, Margaret had asked *her* Gatekeeper to protect us all, and the house. "Protection being a very important step in the proceedings, all you have to do is ask, if you don't ask you don't get!" said Margaret.

Our Instructor began, "You need to visualise, and ask for, a silver jug above your heads, pouring silver liquid over your shoulders and down over your bodies, down over your legs, and over and under you feet, to cover and protect you."

This we did very slowly, visualizing each part of our bodies as they were covered in silver protection.

Margaret continued, "Then taking three deep breaths, you are to 'ground' yourselves by visualizing zips on the bottom of your feet. Now open the zips and allow roots from your feet to grow, then take them to the centre of the earth, again taking three, deep, breaths."

"At the centre of the earth you have your crystal," announced Margaret.

At this point I didn't know what I had! But figured if this was to work I just had to go with the flow.

"Wrap your roots round your crystal, and take three more breaths to come back up," we were told. I was just about still with her.

"Now you are going to 'open up,' came the instruction.

This meant we had to open our chakras. These are the seven main energy points of the body, the same as Reiki uses, these points being the main focus points by which healing energy is brought into the body.

I have enclosed a picture to help illustrate these.

Margaret told us, "The easiest and quickest way to open up, is to imagine the chakras as having buttons and press them on, to open."

This I'd never been shown before. It was brilliant, so quick, rather than waiting for petals of a lotus flower to unfold, as I had been told previously, you just imagine one press on each chakra and it's open.

Everything Margaret had told us so far I could picture, it was so, so clear.

On each chakra we were to take a big breath. I could picture myself pushing each of my buttons and the resulting 'opening up' of the chakra. Apparently pushing them again later, when we had finished, would turn them off and close them down.

So with buttons switched on, each chakra had its own corresponding coloured light that shone into the middle of the room. After this, we were told to visualise a trap door above our heads and on this, a silver bolt. We were to slide the silver bolt across, and allow the trap door to swing open.

At this point, the most beautiful bright, white light shone down over and through our bodies. It felt warm and welcoming, quite amazing.

Next, we were to turn our attention to the lights in the middle of the room.

Things were moving rapidly and I was just about hanging on in there, not wishing to get left behind, my lights had just about appeared.

"Spin them as fast as you can," we were told, "so they form a rainbow, then wrap them three times round the person to your right, then to each person in the room, then three times round yourself and back into the centre of the room." This was to insure we all stayed linked together.

Margaret went on, "When all the chakras are open, I would like you to visualise the green light from the heart chakra as a dense green mist, and for it to fill the room and form a platform.

Step into the mist, and onto the platform, and feel yourself going up through the trap door and onto the Astral Plane."

Oh my God! I thought…. really?

The Astral Plane is through the trap door?

Margaret explained, "We are on what is known as the third dimension and Spirit is on the fourth dimension. By deep breathing, it's possible to raise our vibration to reach a dimension of three –and-a –half. Spirit then lower their vibrations one half a dimension from the fourth, to meet us in the middle at three-and-a-half, and this is where the Astral Plane is."

Now, Dear Reader, the following was something that took me some time to understand but is very important, and I feel before we go any further, you should also know:

In meditation things are presented to you on the Astral Plane, by *your* Guides, in a way *you,* hopefully, will learn to understand.

I stepped onto the platform of green mist that Margaret had spoken about, and felt myself rise up. I was a bit apprehensive about going through the trapdoor, so I popped my head through and then bobbed back down again.

This was weird! Margaret had said nothing about bobbing about. Deciding to try again, I rose back up and looked back down where we had come from (Margaret's sitting room) and noticed it was in darkness. Where we were going was the most beautiful bright sunny day!

Margaret carried on with her instruction; we with our visualization.

"The green mist that brought you up is clearing, and in front of you is a path," Margaret said.

I could see a path with grass on both sides, in front of us.

"Over to the right is a big tree, with another path leading off to the right, towards fields. The main path in front of you is leading down to a waterfall."

This I could clearly hear. I could see a stream to the left that followed the path, we walked on a little way, once past the tree,

Margaret's voice gently directed us, "Go down the grassy bank to the stream, take off your shoes, step onto the flat stones. There are seven stepping-stones across the stream, go across them, then step in behind the waterfall. Once here, you are to face the water and feel it run all over your bodies. This is to make sure you are properly cleansed for a visit to the Astral Plane."

On our walk to the waterfall I could hear the noise of the water getting louder and louder. I thought that the water was going to hurt when I stepped under it, but it felt soft and welcoming. I turned around and cleansed my back and felt refreshed all over. Margaret gave us our final bit of instruction, after this she was to say nothing.

"Retrace your steps across the stepping-stones, up the bank, and go and wait over by the big tree that you passed on you way in. Stand up when your Gatekeepers arrive."

It was at this point Margaret's instruction stopped.

I made my way back from the waterfall as instructed, and wondered if I did, in fact, have any clothes on. I couldn't see myself and I also wondered if there was anyone else wandering around that could see us naked? I didn't feel at all cold, on the contrary, quite warm.

The grass looked as if it had been cut. It was quite short with no weeds, none that I could see anyway!

We did as Margaret had instructed and sat under the tree of knowledge, and waited for our Gatekeepers. We were to stand up and greet them, as this was only polite. Tom and I were roughly about the same distance away from each other in the meditation, as we were in Margaret's sitting room: about 6 ft. Tom was to my left, I couldn't see him properly but felt his presence beside me, and I could 'see' a dark shadow in my peripheral vision.

The sun was strong and this tree was big, a huge oak or chestnut, its branches hanging fairly low, to about a man's height, and it was beautiful. The scene was a summer's day.

As I sat quietly, I was still able to hear the waterfall. Apart from this, the experience was of a wonderful calm, quiet space. I did feel we weren't alone, but I couldn't see anyone, and didn't feel frightened. I was quite excited in fact.

Then out of a white mist at the end of the path, next to where we had emerged from the trapdoor, I saw a figure in a grey cloak. The hood was a big floppy one. I couldn't see its left side properly, but could see a bright, white ball of light flash around it and around the right knee. It seemed as if this figure had emerged from a pathway or platform, but I couldn't see clearly.

The white mist faded as the hooded figure came closer and then I could make out what seemed to be another set of legs….bare legs. The two figures appeared to be speaking or trying to communicate, but I could not make it out.

My eyes made their way up the bare legs to rest on a type of skirt. It then dawned on me that it was, in fact, a Roman soldier; *My* Roman Soldier. I always felt that I had a Roman soldier looking after me. I could not believe it! I wondered if I had just imagined it, and it was imagination taking over.

I looked at him again. He had a leather strap going from his right shoulder to his waist on his left side, and a belt. He had beautiful, strong looking arms and his skin was a lovely olive brown colour, and not a hair in sight on his arms or his legs. Now, *I must* be dreaming!!

I turned my attention to the figure in grey, which I now recognised was silver. Not a highly polished 'bling' but a subtle silver, and I tried to make out the face. I felt the energy was soft but knowledgeable; kind and caring. Was this my Guide or my Gatekeeper? Phew! I really didn't know.

Over to my left where Tom sat, I could sense what I can only describe as a huge form. Not a shadow with a uniform colour, but shades, which I took to be a bush I'd not noticed before on the way in. My attention returned to the figures in front of me, and I felt they were each holding one of my hands. Holding my left hand was the figure in silver, and the soldier held my right. I could not make out my soldier's face, but he was still there. I felt he had something on his head, maybe it was a crown? I wasn't sure.

Margaret had told us to ask their names, what they did and also what they had done on the Earth plane. I tried: "Arthur", came back as clear as a bell, like it was written in front of me. Arthur.

Next, I thought I'd try asking him what he did.

"I clear your path. It's a jungle out there girl!!" came the reply.

It made me smile. Am I really hearing it, or imagining it, or going cuckoo? I didn't know......

"What did you do on Earth?" I asked.

"I was a Roman soldier," he replied.

I didn't know what else to say, so I thanked him silently in my head, with heart- felt sincerity, for everything he had done for me in the past. I thought I had felt him move in on occasions, and now I had confirmation of what I had felt.

I just looked at the pair of them in absolute awe. I was not able to hear anything they were saying, but it was obvious they were conversing. I still couldn't make out any facial features, but I had a sense of great honour to be there, and to meet them. This is the only way I can describe what I felt.... It was all quite 'different'.

Time had gone so fast, as soon as we arrived on the Astral Plane it appeared it was time to leave.

Margaret's voice broke the silence, "You have 5 minutes left."

I really was stuck for things to say to these shadowy figures except:

"Thank you very, very much."

We bid our farewells and walked back down the gravel path to the hatch. To the right of the hatch was standing a beautiful deer. It did not move as we approached, but just kept looking at us.

We stepped back into the green mist and arrived back down into Margaret's sitting room, knowing full well that we had never left. I did hear Margaret leave the room at one point during the meditation, either to cough or sneeze.

It had been a truly wonderful experience, and Tom and I both saw, and then wondered about, things that Margaret hadn't mentioned.

Tom also had seen the figure in the grey cloak, and thought he had two Gatekeepers or Guides as well. Margaret told us that she had been there with us and that we definitely had only one Gatekeeper each.

Who, then, was this other figure we both definitely saw?

Margaret asked her Guide. She was surprised at the answer, because the figure in grey was in fact…. Margaret herself! They had wrapped a sliver cloak around her and she didn't know she had one, but Tom and I both saw it. It was all so amazing!

Now although Margaret had talked us through this meditation from walking the path, the waterfall, and then back to the tree, this is where her instruction had stopped, there were still aspects of the meditation that she hadn't revealed to us, including who our Gatekeepers were going to be.

Margaret had meditated with her Guides the day before and had received all the information about us, and had it already written down.

She revealed that Tom's Gatekeeper was a huge, Mongolian warrior, absolutely massive, whom I had mistaken for a huge bush. She told Tom the name of his Gatekeeper and he seemed overwhelmed by it all. Apparently, his Gatekeeper had sat on him! Tom was humbled by the whole experience, even though, poor chap, he'd been pinned down. Margaret then finally revealed what I had been waiting for: who my Gatekeeper was…… A Roman soldier…! Yes!!! It was **not** my imagination. His name was Artois, or something similar, I didn't quite catch it.

"Oh I got 'Arthur', but I wasn't sure," I said.

I was just thinking I'd got it all wrong when Margaret stopped me.

"Wait a minute," she said, pointing her finger at me.

"Arthur is the English translation of his name."

Well! I can tell you now, I didn't know whether to laugh or cry. What a night!

Margaret then explained that after each meditation we must close down our Chakras.

"First go to your feet and imagine your roots, take three breaths and draw them back in. Next think of your zips on the soles of your feet and pull them closed. Now picture your chakras as buttons on a child's toy and are lit up. Press each one in turn starting with the base chakra which is red and at the bottom of the spine, until all your chakra lights have gone out. Then lastly look above your head and push the trap door closed, and slide the silver bolt across. You are now closed down," Margaret had concluded with a huge smile.

We thanked Margaret profusely, and embarked on our journey home, our heads full of what we had both seen, and shared some of the quite funny and unexpected aspects. Independent of what Margaret had told us, we apparently both shared some of the same concerns.

We both had been apprehensive about going up through the trapdoor at first, not knowing what we would find. Were we clothed when we left the waterfall? We had a giggle about that one.

We both noticed that the grass was trimmed, and both saw the beautiful deer that resembled Bambi, only a lot bigger. It was young and a lovely red colour, with big white spots but no antlers, and lovely big brown eyes.

The whole experience was more than we could ever have possibly imagined and not at all what we expected: not that we had any idea at all, of what to expect.

BALL CLEANSING MEDITATION

12th September 2008

THIS MEDITATION WAS GIVEN TO us by Margaret for some homework. It's a meditation to cleanse all the chakras. The instructions were to open up the chakras the way that Margaret had shown us, using the silver jug etc as before.

This time we were told to ask our Gatekeeper to cleanse the room we were in; the house from the roof down to the footings; basically the whole area, with Universal cleansing energy, and to place waterfalls at the exits (the windows and doors) for protection and to ensure that any negative energy had gone, before we opened up.

Tom was at work on this particular day, and I decided to have a go on my own. After I was sure I had covered all these points, I opened up in the usual way, which I found to be very thorough.

Margaret had said we would see a ball above our heads in our minds eyes. Now I didn't know whether there was going to be a ball over my head or not, but knowing what I had seen at Margaret's house with the first Meditation, anything could be possible.

Anyway, I thought I would give it a go, and looked up for my ball, and there it was! It was moss green in colour, with a little pink centre. I sent it spinning, and then directed it down through all of my chakras. This is what we were told to do, at the heart chakra it needed to stay for a while. I had been experiencing a strange, uncomfortable feeling, almost painful at times, right in the centre of my chest. The ball rested there for a while, still spinning, then moved down my body through each chakra in turn, making them seem a lot brighter, or it could have been that I was more aware of them. I concentrated, and sent the ball down each leg, and then I spun it back the other way, it reached the end of my foot, just as Margaret had instructed, to clean all the debris away. On the way down, I felt my ball was spinning a little off centre, which made me feel like I was wobbling as I did the meditation. Here I was, sat with my eyes shut in our sitting room, and what on earth anyone would have thought had they walked past the house and caught a glimpse of me in the window, I dread to think.

Thankfully the ball seemed to move a lot smoother on the way back up through the chakras. I could sense the ball had turned an orangey- rusty colour as I made it spin up and out of the crown chakra. Yuck! It looked like mud! I glanced up again, and to my surprise, there was another ball, still the same colour, so I sent it down again. This time it travelled down through the chakras a lot smoother and quicker. It was still brown when it exited, but my heart chakra was starting to feel different. The third time I looked up, in my mind's eye, and I saw another ball, but this time it was white. I was expecting to send it down like I had done the other two, then realised that it wasn't a ball, but the pure white light from the trapdoor.

The white light started to descend through my body, stopping at each chakra, almost like switching a light on. The light was filling me up from the top first. Fascinating! As the light reached my feet it felt fantastic, just like it feels when I tune in to a healing treatment and I can feel all of the energy flowing through my hands. It was amazing. My whole body was buzzing with white light. The whole beam suddenly went slimmer, to about the width of my wrist, and then I realised that it was no longer white but gold. Wow!

It was as if the beams had changed my whole body, and had sorted it out and was putting it back together in its rightful place. It felt all contained! I felt quite odd thinking that....

I closed down and realised that my heart chakra had been open for a very long time, and not been shut down properly. I almost felt the chakra creak shut. How I knew this I really don't know, but its how I felt, and now that I had cleansed and closed it properly, it felt really good.

Before I started the meditation, I asked my Gatekeeper for help so that no one was to disturb me, so I could get the job finished. As I finished closing down from the meditation, just as I slid the silver bolt back over my trapdoor, the phone rang, it was Tom with a feeling he should ring me. I was so excited that I just had to tell him what I'd done, and what it felt like, and now he was keen to try as well.

It was fantastic what we were achieving and experiencing. I couldn't quite believe it.

Ball Cleansing Meditation with Tom

15th September 2008

TOM AND I WERE ABOUT to embark on a ball cleansing meditation together. Tom was unsure about which order the chakras and their colours came in, so I read the meditation from a sheet Margaret had given us.

The ball in my mind's eye this time was a different colour. This time the colours were apple- green and Indigo and not so profound. I didn't feel the white light or see the gold colour, but the whole cleansing felt a lot smoother travelling up and down the chakras. The balls still looked a little grubby as they were leaving the crown chakra, though I did feel that stopping to read from a sheet of paper possibly stopped me from tuning in as well as I could have.

It was still a pleasurable experience, and I'm pleased that Tom enjoyed it too. His colours were different to mine. He had a red ball, and after he had finished his cleansing, he did comment that he felt a lot better in himself.

All this work with Margaret got me thinking. How was it going to affect the treatments that I was going to do with my clients? Would

I notice any difference in the energy that I work with? I decided that after working on one of my clients, incorporating the methods that I had learnt from Margaret, I would take a few notes on how I felt at the end of the treatment.

The first treatment I gave after the first Meditation with Margaret was a Hara massage. This helps reduce emotional stress and is very effective.

My client was due in the afternoon, so I asked my Gatekeeper for protection, for everything; the treatment room; the whole house; the garden. I also remembered to ask for myself, and to ask for all Guides, mine and my clients, to be present at 2.30.

My client had been going through a tough time, leaving her emotionally exhausted and stressed. When she arrived, I asked for my Guides and healers to be present so that they may send the appropriate healing energy

As I started to work on the lady's feet, with my eyes shut, I looked up into my mind's eye and saw the trapdoor. My breathing had deepened and I felt relaxed and tuned in. I saw myself standing in a room with a low ceiling, and at the far end of the room I could make out a small crowd of about eight to twelve people whom I didn't recognise. They were all standing quietly and looking towards me. It was weird.

The lady was lying on the mat in my treatment room, and I could see the white light coming down, almost like it was in a theatre, and the room seemed unusually dark.

This was all happening in my treatment room with my eyes closed. Normally the treatment room is quite light.

Suddenly in the background behind the crowd, with head and shoulders visible above everyone else, was standing the most enormous, beautiful brown Bear. I started to chuckle as I'd never seen anything like it. He was stood on his hind legs looking around and at the crowd. He was observing them, or was it that I was the one being observed? He was passive, and looked completely at ease and I think, yes, he looked happy. He reminded me of the Bear from the

Jungle Book, with the most beautiful, velvety brown coat and a tan coloured muzzle. Wow! He stayed with me for the whole treatment and I really wasn't sure if he was for my client or myself.

I didn't know the woman well enough to tell her, and even then…. Best keep that one to myself I thought! The treatment appeared to be a success, and she seemed more relaxed and said that she felt uplifted and a lot better than when she arrived.

Maybe she had seen a Bear too.?!

A heart Chakra healing and a Meditation with Margaret

1ˢᵗ October 2008

IT WAS TWO WEEKS SINCE our first visit to Margaret's house. The journey down had an air of excitement. Tom and I were like two small children chatting nineteen to the dozen about how eager we were to see Margaret, and anticipating what the evening may have in store for us.

Previously I had mentioned to Margaret on the phone about a pain in my chest, where the heart chakra is, and she had told me that she would do some healing on it. She had spoken to Sheryle, and was told to tell me to put silver discs over the chakra at the front and back, as Sheryle believed that I was leaking energy.

What I needed to do was to place my hand over my heart chakra, and ask Spirit to place shields over it. I visualised this, but they appeared to turn gold.

"Not to worry," Margaret said, "mine did the same when I had to do it."

"How big is the disc on your back?" Margaret asked.

"It's huge!" I said. "Just like a shield".

"Well, put them on front and back and we'll talk about it when you arrive," and we left it like that.

When we reached Margaret's house she welcomed us in, and informed me that she had spoken to her Guide and to Sheryle, about my condition, and apparently the first thing she had to do was undertake a repair on my heart chakra.

The chakra was large and had three tears, Margaret said, and this was because I worked from the heart, and put it into everything I did.

The chakra was also having trouble shutting down properly and needed to be repaired and shrunk down to the correct size. Margaret put one hand on my chest and placed the other on my back, and then started to make circular movements.

My bra was killing me, it was far too tight, and so I asked if I could loosen it.

"Of course you can," she laughed, and then she hit me on the arm.

"It's not your bra, it's *Them* shrinking it! Can you feel it all tightening up?" Margaret asked.

"Yes!" I replied, and we laughed. (I had loosened my bra the last time we had had a Meditation. Well, she did say get nice and comfy! The damn thing was far too tight and I couldn't breathe!)

After it was done I felt so much better, and thanked Margaret. It was all accomplished so quickly.

"Well," she said with a twinkle in her eye, "They use all sorts of modern things you know; glue as well!."

It definitely felt different, and the pain had gone.

Margaret explained about energy, and showed Tom and me an exercise. We were to learn how to feel each other's energy. Tom stood at the far end of the room and we put our hands up, palms facing forward towards each other. Margaret asked Tom to move forwards then backwards. I could actually feel his energy. It felt stronger, then weaker. Amazing! We swapped places and Tom got the chance to feel my energy. He could feel mine just as I had felt his. Then it was Margaret's turn. I hinted that we would probably feel hers from the car park at the end of the road. "You could feel Sheryle's from there I expect," she laughed.

After our energy awareness exercise, I felt quite strange. I felt that Tom's energy was all kind of spiky, whereas Margaret's energy was soft like velvet, similar to the energy I have felt from gold. Hers was beautiful and I said as much. "That's light energy," she said, and then invited us to join her in the kitchen for a break and a cuppa.

At this point in these journals that I am writing, and before sharing the next meditation with you dear reader, I think it is about time I explained something about Tom. He has always been able to see 'auras'. These are the colourful energy fields that surround every living thing. I had not known this about Tom until one day, after about twenty-three years of marriage, he decided to tell me of this skill. I had absolutely no idea, Tom had always kept it quiet, and when I asked him more about it, he simply said, "It wasn't the sort of thing that blokes discuss," and had always thought that it was something everyone could see.

Our second working Meditation with Margaret was to meet our Spirit Guides, so after we had finished our cup of tea, we moved back into Margaret's sitting room and sat ourselves down. Tom sat in the same place as before, at the far end of the sofa, and I sat in Margaret's comfy chair in the corner, with Margaret on my right. Tom then shifted his position to the middle of the sofa. "I've been told to shove up unless I want to get sat on again," he grinned.

We started the Meditation in the usual way, by grounding, protecting and opening up our chakras. I felt as if there was someone sitting beside me on my right (in addition to Margaret) beside my right shoulder.

"I can feel a presence, someone is next to me," I told Margaret.

She just smiled at me and carried on talking us through the meditation!

As we ascended through the trap door, I felt it was a bit overcrowded: Tom with his massive Gatekeeper, Margaret with hers and me with Arthur.

When I felt I had arrived on the Astral Plane, I looked around and saw that everything was the same as it had been before. The tree was just as big, the fields, the river, and the waterfall were all there and in the same place. The only slight difference was that it all looked a little hazy, not as clear. I walked along the gravel path, kicking off my shoes quickly, as Margaret was now talking us over the stepping-stones and I hadn't quite got there yet.

Margaret's step-by-step instruction stopped here.

She had told us over our cuppa that when we approached the waterfall today, and after cleansing ourselves in the waterfall, we were to turn with our backs to it, and look into the cave behind it where there would be something that she wished us to find.

Cave? What cave? I didn't see a cave last time!

I turned round after letting the water cleanse my front; I could hear it and feel it running down my back. Sure enough there was a cave, and peering in, it appeared very dark .Then out of the darkness I could see a shape. It was white in colour or maybe lit up in some way. At the top, it became thinner and pointed, and at the base it was roundish. It reminded me of an ornament that could be found in a church, and I felt that maybe it could be sacred. Studying it harder, I could see that it was carved in and out, and resembled a pepper pot grinder or even a table leg. On the top was a ball which reached skyward in a point. I had no idea what it was. Then I picked up on a church candle, one of the short, dumpy ones.

This is roughly what I saw, though I think the picture on the right may have been a little bit wider.

Prior to the meditation, Margaret had directed us that when we had seen what we were allowed to see, we should exit the cave, and make our way back over the stepping stones and over to the tree.

I wasn't sure, but I thought I could sense someone present on my left by the embankment, as I was walking to the tree. I couldn't see anything, I just had a feeling.

Both Tom and I were to sit under the tree, but not directly on top of each other. At this point I couldn't see him clearly, and he seemed about the same distance away as we were in Margaret's front room.

I looked all around to see everything that I could, and thought I saw coloured ducks with yellow feet, by the river.

I didn't know why I couldn't see as clearly as the last time. Maybe it was due to tiredness or just trying too hard.

I had a fleeting glimpse of Margaret in her cloak by the trapdoor where we had come from. She seemed to be obscured somewhat, by what appeared to be Tom's visitors who had come to greet him. I couldn't see very much at all, it was at best only vague shapes to me, and looked like a huge totem pole. Some kind of mist was surrounding them as well, which made it even cloudier.

Then I thought I was being nosey, and that these visitors weren't for me, and maybe I was not meant to see them anyway.

So to my left I couldn't see a thing, but sat patiently for my Guide to come. I kept looking around, as Margaret had told me to do. I looked up in the tree and saw a blackbird. Tom told me later that he had seen a lovely blue bird. I was a little envious as I'd only seen an old crow! Then I wondered if it was my mind playing tricks or if I was suffering from an over- active imagination, because my Guide still hadn't appeared. Perhaps the bird had been put in the tree for me to have something to look at, or maybe just to keep me happy. I loved to see birds in our garden.

Then out of the corner of my eye I thought I saw a little brown mouse running across the grass and through the leaves in front of me. Suddenly it ran off to the right and disappeared.

Everything was really fuzzy now, and I wasn't seeing anything too clearly in front of me. It was like the interference on a television when it's not tuned in properly, only it wasn't a television it was here, right in front of my face! I tried looking around the fuzz, and noticed there seemed to be a small gap between Tom's entourage and the fuzzy bit.

Having another look around, I found I could see to my right, and could just pick out a white cloak and a man with dark hair. Here he is, at last! I had honestly thought my Guide had given up.

"Hello," I said. "My name is Grace."

The name Peter came through to me, as clear as a bell. He still stood well to the side and seemed reluctant to come closer.

Then, from out of nowhere, I felt the most wonderful cuddle. It was a beautiful, loving energy that completely engulfed my back and arms. I had a feeling that my right hand was being held and maybe my left as well, but I wasn't sure. I also thought I had caught a glimpse of Philip, who during my childhood, was like a second dad to me.

He had sadly passed away, at the age of 52, but here he came and went in a flash. With that, another face came into view. It was the face of a beautiful young lady, like a cameo picture that was being shown me. She had dark shoulder length hair, with small features and olive skin. She was tiny. And then she was gone. And then I was back with Peter.

I was straining to concentrate and get more detail on him, but was still not able to see very clearly in front of me. I started to feel a bit crowded in.

Tom's lot to my left were still obscuring my view of that side, and the feeling of not being able to see in front of me started to make me feel a little annoyed and disappointed, to be honest. I had no idea if the gentleman to my right was mine or not, but I was still experiencing this warm comforting hug, so I guessed he must be. I had felt he was trying to communicate something to me, but what, I had no idea. I couldn't hear his voice or see his lips, so again I wasn't convinced.

Margaret suddenly spoke, "You have five minutes."

Oh No! I thought.

I hadn't asked any questions except for his name, and Margaret had told us to talk to our Guides. This was hardly talking. I expect he thought he'd 'got a right one here!' My mind went completely blank. I couldn't think of one question or one thing to say. I thought maybe I'd better show I had manners ,and thanked him so very much for everything he had done for me, though I really wasn't sure what he **had** done, it just felt the polite thing to do.

"Well?" Margaret asked. "How was that?"

I looked across at Tom who looked dazed, and said he could feel tears on his face, but they weren't his.

Margaret turned and looked at me. "Well?"

I took a deep breath and conveyed everything I had seen …or not seen, from when I was sat under the tree.

"My Guide, I think, is a man called Peter." I said.

"No," Margaret replied. "Your Guide is Marie-Anne, she is a nun dressed in a grey habit. She is small, about your height with a hat." (Margaret had given me the correct name for the hat but I can't recall it.)

"Peter," she carried on,"is Sheryle's Guide. He may have come to have a look at you," she smiled and added, "Your Guide Marie-Anne is of the Clair Order. She is from France and lived until she was 81 years old. She died in the early 1900s. She brings you peace and calmness and she is a healer. She also worked in an orphanage. You felt her presence, which is good."

I still thought it was all very exciting but was experiencing slight disappointment at not being able to see Marie-Anne.

"Well," Margaret grinned looking at me, "Everything about his lot is huge!" Margaret said, nodding in Tom's direction.

Tom then went on to explain about how he had seen a white horse on a plateau above the waterfall, calmly eating grass. It was so white, it almost looked false, but then the tallest knight he had ever seen appeared, dressed in chain mail with a white tunic. He was a towering seven feet tall, slim built.

"His name is William and he is a Cathar knight." Margaret said.

Tom had picked up on the name Abraham but like me, couldn't hear too well. "Well, I got the end of the name…am," Tom said.

He also thought he saw his mother, his grandfather, and my dad, and they were all waving at him from a distance. I was really surprised that Tom had seen my dad. I hadn't seen anything like that, and I hadn't asked any questions either. I felt a bit sorry for myself, although it was all still fascinating, really fascinating.

Margaret was thrilled with our efforts. The object in the cave was her staff with a crystal ball on the top. Apparently she had put it in the cave, a long way back and got the Spirits to put the same silver around it as they had done with her cloak on the first Meditation, so that we would know it related to her. Neither of us had managed to get that part of it. Nevertheless, she was chuffed that we had picked up on what we had. The candle was also hers.

The three of us made arrangements to meet again, in another two weeks time, Tom and I said our thanks and goodbyes.

Tom later confirmed, on our drive home, that he saw Margaret's aura as a beautiful silver colour, which was probably why everything on the Astral Plane relating to her was bathed in silver, though to be quite honest, this connection took us ages to work out. Also, as we were chatting in the car on the way home, I expressed sadness at not being able to see Marie-Anne and my dad, although my father and I were never that close when he was alive, but I considered him, through his actions when we were growing up, to be probably one of my best teachers.

He taught me never to expect anything from anyone.

I felt he himself never felt the need to do a lot with me, or with either of my sisters, or even my brother, when we were young, or any other time, come to think of it!

I could be wrong of course, I viewed it through a child's eye. The only time he showed any emotion was when Tom and I got married and there was a tear in his eye.

"Come on then girl," he said, as we made our way to the registry office. Everyone else had gone ahead and it was just the two of us.

I never knew his views or feelings on anything, and the only time he ever seemed to speak to us, was to tell us off. So I can honestly say that the day he died I realised that I never really knew my dad, even though we lived in the same house until I was seventeen and moved out.

As the car continued down the road, a wave of sadness came over me. Was it the thought of dad still being on the outside of things, not ever joining in, and now not having friends or us, his family, around him?

In my mind's eye I could picture him.

To explain this, if I was to say to you now "What does your house look like?" You can picture it right now in *your* minds' eye. This is how I saw him.

He was dressed in navy trousers and a checked shirt with a blue tank top, which he often wore.

"That's right," Tom said. "That's what he was wearing".

I could see him clearly and could see him waving to me. Tears started to roll down my face. Was this because I could now see him, all alone, or because I was missing the grumpy old sod?

"Those are the tears I felt," Tom said.

A Little Reflection

THE NEXT DAY TOM AND I chatted some more.

"My knight arrived on a white horse," Tom proudly announced.

Then it dawned on me why I had not seen Marie-Anne. I was waiting for her to arrive in the same manner that Arthur had done, watching him walk towards me. Marie-Anne had in fact been with me all the time. She had been stood at my right shoulder, in Margaret's sitting room, and it was her presence I had felt beside me as I went up through the trapdoor. Yes. She had been with me all the time! No wonder I had felt that it was overcrowded. She didn't have to arrive because she was already with me, and because I hadn't seen her arrive, I didn't stand up to greet her properly. She had walked from behind and had stood right in front of me. The television interference that I thought I was looking at was, in fact, the fuzziness of her grey habit that I was trying to look through. She must have thought me so very rude, there I was, trying to look around her or through her, and there she was, right in front of me all the time.

Toms' Guide had announced his arrival with a white charger. Mine arrived 'as quiet as a mouse'....or as quiet as a church mouse. The brain cogs were going into overdrive...nun... church, the mouse I'd seen......

Both Tom and I laughed; the Guides had been so very, very clever with their clues.

My own Meditation

October 5ᵗʰ 2008

After the slight disappointment of last Wednesday, and not 'seeing' my Guide, I felt as if I needed to apologise to Marie-Anne and see if I could speak with her.

I started to ground myself, opened up and cleansed myself. The balls this time were orange and then yellow. I asked for Marie-Anne to come and speak to me. Shortly after asking, I felt her comforting presence, and asked if it would be possible for me to see her face. I could make out the face of a nun, but it wasn't very clear.

"It's clearer on the Astral Plane. Would you like to come up?" she asked.

Gosh! I thought. The idea certainly appealed to me, but what if I couldn't come back down, or started seeing things I didn't wish to see?

I had cleansed the house, garden, cars, and absolutely everything I could think of in our plot. Ok here goes, I thought.

"Will you stay with me Marie-Anne, and can Arthur come too please?" I asked. She agreed, so off we went.

Up on the Astral Plane, I cleansed myself in the waterfall, but was still aware of something on the embankment from last time. I walked over to the tree where Marie-Anne was already waiting for me. This time, I thought I would stay standing all of the time.

I could see my dad on the plateau above the waterfall, still dressed the same as the other day. Marie-Anne asked if I'd like him to come over and speak with me, so I said yes, and then in a flash, here he was, standing next to me. He appeared at my side so very quickly and it felt strange. I felt that he was smiling and wishing to hold my hand. I noticed that his energy was different to Marie-Anne's. Hers had a warm, velvety feel to it, whereas my dad's was cooler and not so dense. His hair was blonde and curly. He appeared to have lost weight and looked a lot younger.

Towards the end of his life, my dad had ended up with hardly any hair, and it was odd seeing him before me with a full head.

He came with love, wishing to say hello. I felt quite emotional.

"You needed to do this meeting on your own," Marie-Anne told me. I could see her face. This time she appeared to me as a more mature lady, not the young nun that I had seen before. Her face appeared rounder, with a pale complexion and red cheeks. Was this the same person but older, or someone completely different? Thoughts were flying through my head and I didn't know for sure who it was.

Dad said he was fine and sent his love to me and for me to tell mum that he was ok, and to send his love to her too. The grumpy figure that I remembered him to be was now gone, and standing before me was a man happy to see me, proud to see me, and I got the feeling that at some point he had known he would see me again, and that I would get to see him. I couldn't get over the fact that both figures before me felt totally different to be around.

Margaret had informed us that if we ventured up onto the Astral Plane ourselves, we would know when it was time to leave, and just as I was feeling that maybe now was the time to say my goodbyes, this huge vapour/ mist / energy I don't know quite know what to call it, was lifting me, like a shell was gone, a massive weight being lifted from my body. All the uncertainty and fuzziness surrounding my body had dissolved, leaving me feeling solid and secure. I felt lighter, even slimmer with all the unwanted baggage I had accumulated being removed. It was a wonderful feeling. I gave dad a hug, and with a tear in my eye, thanked him for coming and knew it was not going to be the last time we would meet.

Walking down the gravel path to the green mist that had now formed, I could sense a butterfly in my hair. I had been set free.

Reflecting on my meditation the following day, I had a feeling that I no longer had to apologise for my presence in my father's company. I suppose I had spent half of my life apologising for who I was, and now I realised that actually, I ***do*** have a right to ***be***.

MARGARET'S ADVICE

I FELT IT WAS TIME FOR me to get my house in order, so to speak. After all, if I was going to help others, it was important for me to help myself.

In my past, I had encountered difficulties with a person who, although was no longer playing a part in my life, still had some kind of emotional hold over my thoughts and feelings from time to time, and it was hard for me to move on from her hold. I had told Margaret about this situation.

She had mentioned that it might be a good idea to ask Marie-Anne to help release this person's grip on me.

I duly asked for her help and Marie-Anne showed me a totally different picture from the one I had painted in my mind. This was an important day for me.

I went to the Astral Plane and met Marie-Anne.

"Look to your left beyond the tree, and out to the field," Marie-Ann said.

I could see rabbits bouncing around, eating grass and chasing each other. Then a big, brown, shire horse in brasses came into view, looking grand, as it ploughed the field. Being in reins it was held in a strict line, not able to wavier. But no one was holding the reins!

"This is how this woman sees herself," explained Marie -Anne,

"As having an important job to do, she sees herself as an important workhorse and has given herself a major task, which she must be seen to do alone. She has chained herself down in doing this, and cannot or does not wish to break free; she likes to be seen as a martyr. She sees you as a rabbit, playing at what you do, and having a life with little strain. This she finds annoying and would like to crush you beneath her feet. You have fun, and seem not to have worked for it............ in her eyes.

She then tries to draw on everyone around her to lighten the burden she has made for herself. In doing this, she tires, drains, and steals their energy. She is actually weakening her gifts, which in turn, makes her task more difficult to accomplish. It is a downward spiral: only she can get herself out of it. Kick up your heels, and find pastures new, Grace, as this situation is not helping you one bit. You will not move forward otherwise. She is too full of her own importance."

It got me thinking, and over a couple of days 'the penny dropped' and I realised what I had to do. Until now, I had allowed this person to convince me that I knew nothing, and what little I did know, wasn't worth much. She, on the other hand, presented herself as far superior. This was always going to hold me back in life, but what I needed to do was to release this damaging thought. This person was no longer in my life, so it was literally the thought that constantly had me in an iron grip, holding me back. It was time to let go of that thought. So, once again, in a matter of days, I had set myself free and waved goodbye to more unwanted baggage.

A Short Meditation at Home

9th October 2008

IN THIS MEDITATION, THE JOURNEY took me firstly to the cave behind the waterfall. The usual cleansing and protection had already taken place, so here I was, looking as far inside the back of the cave as I could. Previously, I thought I had caught a glimpse of a crystal or two, which I love, and this time just by looking a little more closely, I could see that they were everywhere. It was a beautiful sight, but I did have a feeling it was not permitted to fully enter the cave at this point in time, and after all, I did have other things I wished to ask Marie-Anne, so I hot-footed it back over the stepping stones to the tree, to talk to her.

After we had finished chatting, I looked over and saw my dad waving at me from the same place as before.

"Do you wish for him to join us?" asked Marie-Anne.

"Yes please," I replied, and as before, he was at my side in an instant. This time his face appeared clearer. His eyes were a deep blue and not like the old pale coloured eyes that I looked into just before he passed away. The same thick, curly blonde hair that I saw the last time was prominent, and he caught hold of my hand. I wanted to ask more questions, but then I realised dad was talking. How rude of me, I thought. Here he was, making an effort to come all this way to communicate with me, and here I was, waffling on about my own trivial stuff. I apologised and he told me that it was ok.

"I just wanted to come to tell you that I love you very much, and that you make me very proud," he said. I was thrilled. He seemed so much lighter, and behaved in an almost jocular manner. It was odd. Now it felt so natural to have a conversation with him. I felt I could chat to him at any time and on any day. It almost felt that I was taking his presence for granted, and that he just lived down the road. He asked me to send his love to my sister Claire, and to keep an eye on her.

It was time for me to go. Marie-Anne's face was still getting clearer, but I could not see Arthur's face very clearly.

The deer that Tom and I had both previously seen was there again, but what significance it was we still hadn't found out.

I returned to the green mist and started to descend, with thoughts still resting on my dad being 'up there', and so I returned with a *bump!* I must concentrate more, I thought, and then as I looked back up to the trapdoor, Dad poked his head back down and was laughing and waving at me.

I thanked everyone for helping me and it felt really good to have put everything back in order, and to straighten out parts of my life. I certainly felt so much better for it.

CRYSTALS

15ᵗʰ October 2008

THIS WAS OUR THIRD MEETING with Margaret and both Tom and I were very excited. She has such a lovely character and a wicked sense of humour, so we found learning with her very enjoyable. Her down- to -earth approach to things makes everything seem so easy, which only goes to prove what a talented teacher she is. This in turn rubs off onto us, her students, and makes us feel we can achieve our goals. Unfortunately for Margaret, I have days when my brain is full of cotton wool and even for her it must seem to be a monumental task to get anything through to me. What patience, bless her!

Margaret listened to our reports and about my visit to the Astral Plane. She was chuffed that I was able to communicate with Marie-Anne. I had previously spoken to Margaret on the phone, telling of the meditation that led to me meeting my dad, and how her words of wisdom regarding my past problem had at last been understood by me and finally made sense.

I asked Margaret if she could have another go at healing my heart chakra. Even though it had improved, I still occasionally got twinges in my chest. She agreed to help. This time the tightening in my chest, as she worked on me, was a lot more pronounced. On each breath I took I could feel the affected area pull tighter and tighter.

"When the chakra is closed down it should be the size of a golf ball," she said. When Margaret had finished, I thanked her and gave her a hug.

"We must do both your and Tom's auras. Sheryle was going to come over and help. They have to be shrunk down to the right size. When you sleep at night you leave your body, and if you wake with a start, it increases the aura size. If you wake up naturally, you gracefully return to your body and all is fine," Margaret told us. "Being woken up with sharp noises which make you jump, is not good. Hopefully, when Sheryle comes next time, that's what we'll do."

Tom and I smiled at each other. We both knew we'd be in for a night to remember, and couldn't wait until next time!

For this evening, Tom and I settled ourselves down in our usual positions on Margaret's chairs, and she asked if we would like to open ourselves up in the usual way. Tom asked if he could be reminded, as he had difficulty remembering the chakra colours in the right order, and I thought I'd probably take too long, so Margaret decided to talk us through each stage once again.

On reaching the Astral Plane, we were instructed to look behind ourselves this time, when we emerged through the trapdoor, to see if we could see a bridge. This bridge, we were told, would lead us off to an Indian village. If we could see it, there was a possibility that we might be ready to visit it.

Before we could do this, we were told to look into the cave, after we had cleansed ourselves in the waterfall, to see what was there. Margaret then told us we would see crystals.

"I've seen them!" I exclaimed, "Last week! Wow!!" I was beside myself with excitement. "It was when I went up to have a chat with Marie-Anne. It was fantastic!. The whole entrance was full of colours!"Margaret just looked at me and smiled.

You know that putting- foot- in- mouth problem? Well, tonight was one of those moments. Say no more, mouth zipped. Well, it was all just so exciting!

Margaret's instructions were to enter the cave and have a good look around at the layout. We would find a mat which we were to pick up and sit on beside the crystal that took our fancy, and we were to wait for our Guides to arrive.

They would have something to show us. Tom and I took three deep breaths and started on our meditation.

Once through the trapdoor, I could sense that the mist was clearing. I did as I was told and looked behind to see if I could see the bridge. Yes, it was there. One side of it was white; the other side brown.

I looked around and saw that Tom was way down the path, and Margaret's commentary had already taken us to the waterfall. I ran down the path and across the stones, hoping I wouldn't slip and fall. I couldn't help giggling as I raced to catch up. I went under the waterfall, quickly cleansed, and into the cave. I could see the crystals. It was wonderful. I felt like a child in a sweet shop: I didn't know where to look first. I rummaged around for my mat which was a light, neutral kind of colour and resembled a doormat, but when I picked it up half of it turned bright green. Hang on, I thought, now the whole mat has turned green. I felt a panic coming on. I had yet to choose my crystal, and I had a troublesome mat!

It was fantastic. The crystals were all as beautiful as each other. There was a huge amethyst, like half an egg, then every colour of the rainbow. On the left hand side the crystals were laid in rows, almost resembling a rainbow. On the floor there were illuminated white stones.

All of a sudden I remembered Marie-Anne. Where was she? Was she here with me? Oh no! Did I miss her entrance? Was I supposed to meet her by the tree?

Panic was rising. I couldn't remember a darn thing Margaret had told me.

"Marie-Anne," I called in my head, "Marie-Anne!"

"Yes my child," came the calm reply.

I breathed a sigh of relief and sat quickly on my mat, not wanting to get left behind. I was not able to see in full, all the way round the cave. I could pick out Tom and his Guide William in one corner, but I had difficulty trying to make out what else was there. It was difficult to see, and worse, I still had the impossible choice of trying to decide which crystal I wanted, as they were all so lovely. Then, out of the corner of my eye, I could see a row of blue ones, so quickly I put myself and my mat next to them.

Marie-Anne began to show me images. I started to see pictures of the old house I had lived in as a child: me playing in the back garden; when I started work, getting ready in the kitchen in the mornings; getting married; my children playing; up to the present day in our present house. Was this all about my past, present, and maybe future? I couldn't see the future, but maybe suggestions of a log cabin that we were thinking about? I had forgotten to ask questions as Margaret had instructed us to. Were there particular questions? I just could not remember. Then it was time to go. I had definitely fluffed it up this time. Fancy not asking questions!

We both bid our farewells and made our way back towards the waterfall, along the stones, and back onto the path. Dad was again on the plateau waving to me. I waved back. Our trip this time had seemed so quick.

Along the other side of the river I could see bushes. I wondered if they were the ones Tom had seen before, on one of his meditations. He seemed to pick up so much more detail, and a lot quicker, than me.

I saw white flowers and what looked like more grass. The bridge that I had seen earlier was in front of me, and now had flowers growing on each side of it. We walked into the mist and descended to the familiarity of Margaret's sitting room.

"Well?" grinned Margaret. "Grace, what colour was your mat?"

"Err, bright green," I replied

"And yours Tom?" she enquired

"Well it was a bit strange," he said, "it was dark green, but then when I picked it up it had orange lights or orange flecks in it, then the whole mat turned completely orange."

"Well, that's what I wrote down in my notes this morning," she told him.

"What about your crystal Grace?" she asked. "I don't know, what are you like?! You just couldn't decide could you? You were making so much noise giggling. What were you laughing at, when you first went into the cave?"

I explained that I was laughing because I was so late getting to the cave, after being left behind, and told Margaret that eventually I had decided to choose a blue crystal that was similar to the one in my treatment room.

Tom saw loads, and chose a green crystal that seemed to pulsate at him.

"Yes," Margaret affirmed, "but for Grace I put out a pink one."

I don't know if I saw a pink one. There were bright red ones near the roof of the cave, and there seemed to be every colour in there, so it must have been a pink one, but I just didn't see it.

Margaret then asked what I thought Marie-Anne had shown me. I explained about the pictures of my past and present, but didn't know what any of it meant.

"Could it have been this?" she asked, and showed me a word she had written in her book. It said 'Pathways'.

"Would you say that was a good description?" she smiled

I thought about it and thought well yes, I suppose it was. They were my pathways.

Tom was shown different images. First, he was shown a picture of his mum and grandmother on the beach, then a picture of Indian chief Geronimo. After those, he was shown images of many aircraft, looking like bombers. The next sequence was of the Atomic bomb explosion at Hiroshima. There were also pictures of modern day warships. His pictures were on a huge scale, absolutely massive.

Margaret went on to explain that these pictures were of pathways too. Mine was a personal one: Tom's a global one, and that for every pathway in life, there is a choice to be made.

"That, "she said, "was our lesson for tonight."

THE ROOM

29th October 2008

THIS TIME OUR VISIT TO Margaret's home also included a special treat for us: Sheryle was joining us for the Meditation.

This time Margaret did not prepare us with a task. We opened up and cleansed ourselves, then took the familiar steps over to the tree of knowledge.

"Look out for a door in the trunk of the tree. Go through it, down the steps, along the corridor. You will see lots of doors. Choose a door and go inside, "Margaret instructed.

I walked past one door not too sure of the number on it. I kept walking and passed a door which I think may have had a number etched into it; again I wasn't sure. I continued walking and then thought I saw a door with a Reiki symbol on it. I took this as my cue to enter. I asked Marie-Anne if she could make the room brighter, as it was very dark and difficult for me to see, and I didn't want to miss anything this time. The room brightened to reveal its contents. I saw what I thought was a goblet. It had a glow around it and was sat on a big sturdy, wooden table, or was it a bench? To the left I saw a shield which was huge. There wasn't any fancy decoration on it, in fact it was fairly plain looking, but with a big 'bubble' in the middle. It was paired with a heavy looking sword. Actually, there were several swords, and between them and the bench was a suit of armour, and a chain mail hooded top with sleeves, hanging on what looked like a mannequin. It was quite difficult to see to the right, so I stepped further inside the room. I could now make out a glass cabinet with a crown and a cloak, both looking rather regal. The cloak was red in colour and had a fur collar with gems in it. Wow! I thought to myself. It all looked fantastic. The garments were lit up like they were in a showcase in a museum, or like the crown jewels in the Tower of London. The crown was about two inches high with stones inset. I knew that these artefacts were definitely not to be touched. I glanced over to the right of the bench and could see even more swords. There were thin ones and machete types. Above the swords, I could make out some old fashioned pistols. The room seemed to be crammed full, and I was desperately trying to see everything. I looked back over to the left and I picked up on another sword that seemed to be made of wood, and a huge African shield. Next to it was a stand holding African spears, and situated behind that was a dresser, possibly a Welsh dresser, with shelves crammed with random objects and bits of paper. It was difficult to take it all in.

Then, out of the blue, I heard someone whisper in my left ear, "Cuddly toy."

With that, I suddenly saw a large teddy Bear and a conveyor belt, just like the one on the Generation Game years ago on the TV with Bruce Forsyth. I started giggling. Not now! I told myself.

I felt I was behaving like a naughty child giggling in church. This was no laughing matter, Sheryle was here and I didn't want to mess things up. However, the more I tried to focus and be serious about the whole thing, the more this voice kept piping up," Cuddly toy on the conveyor belt tonight."

I felt that my giggles were going to burst out any minute, and it was getting really difficult to contain myself. I simply couldn't allow my giggling to mess up everyone else's meditation, as I had no idea what the others were seeing.

"The Bear is for the children," I heard, and then Margaret's voice interrupted just in time, telling us we had five minutes left and for us to ask our Guide what all the information we had gathered, actually meant.

"Marie-Anne, what is all of this?" I asked.

"This is all for your protection, the whole room is for you," she replied.

I thought how nice it was, then an uneasy thought entered my head: if I needed all of this protection, what on earth was I going to be doing or meeting with later on?

As I left the room I spotted a huge, pink crystal that had been placed on the bench. This, too, was lit up. It reminded me of a similar beautiful crystal I have at home which has a wonderful soft energy surrounding it. . This crystal was beautiful too, but time had run out and I needed to leave the room behind. I thanked Marie-Anne and carried on my way, out into the corridor to join the others, and we all made our way, in a big gang, to the trapdoor.

Back down from our Meditation, and once again in Margaret's sitting room, she smiled and asked me what I had seen. I told her of the door and the contents of the room. Her notes revealed that she had me down for entering door number 3, which had a circle on it. Actually I did enter door number three but I saw a series of circles.

What I had thought was a goblet, that she had put for me to find, was in fact a silver jug, so on the whole I was pleased that our visions were similar. She was very pleased with me, and I was thrilled to think that this week I had got most of it right. The information Margaret had received from her Guide, and written in her book, was similar to what I reported. The crown and cloak I had seen belonged to Margaret, and the cuddly toy, a teddy Bear, was mine.

I told Margaret how beautiful he was and how he would be lovely to cuddle.

"What is your power animal Grace?" she asked.

I didn't think I knew that bit! She reminded me of the treatment I had done, when I had seen a Bear.

Oh! I didn't realize he was mine!

Margaret started laughing, "What are you like?"

We had a good chuckle and Margaret went on to explain that Spirits have a good sense of humour, and that the Bear was for my protection.

"There is a lot of protection surrounding you, as there are three paths that you are following at the moment. The Thai massage, Reiki, and what you are doing with us here. The protection you have is needed for all three."

Tom's Meditation was totally different to mine, and as each of our Meditations are becoming more personal and are leading us down different pathways, I feel that it is for Tom to decide whether his journey is for his eyes only, or to share.

Sheryle had come to join us to check our auras, as Margaret had told us on our last visit. Margaret was right about Tom's, his was huge. He was told to sit down in the middle of the room whilst Sheryle proceeded to walk in circles around him, pausing now and then to speak with her Guide.

"Hmmm, your aura is big and I'm not to touch it, but to leave it as it is. It's meant to be like that. Between the different aura layers, you have rods to hold them out. This I've never seen before, "she told Tom. She then went on to explain that Tom's aura is so big because he is an Earth healer, and can heal the Earth just by his presence. He is also a Soul Rescuer, and as I mentioned earlier, has a talent to see auras.

I guess I always knew he was that little bit special.

Next, it was my turn. Sheryle circled me, putting her hand into my personal energy field. She was standing about eight feet away from where I was sitting, and I could feel a tickling sensation that sent a shiver up my back.

"I'm sorry," she said with a grin.

"You also have a huge aura, and what can only be described as a stubborn streak."

This made Tom's day, and he nodded emphatically in agreement.

"I'm not stubborn!" I protested, but I could feel a smile spreading across my face.

"No, not stubborn, but determined," Sheryle corrected, then added, "When you are with Tom, your aura grows bigger, and when you are not together it shrinks back." She decided that she wasn't to touch mine either.

And so after a cup of tea and saying our thanks and goodbyes, we left Margaret's with our heads full of new experiences and knowledge about ourselves.

A Meditation like no other

FOR THIS NEXT MEDITATION I feel I have to explain, as I did at the beginning of the book, how it works when someone visits the Astral Plane. Consider for a moment, if *you* were going to visit 'up there'. It would be *your* Guide, who works with *you*, giving you information and images, in language which *you* would understand; using your personal worldly knowledge and experiences as the basis for interpreting all that is presented on the Astral Plane. ***It's the interpretation*** that is the ***key*** thing, and ***that is the difficult bit*** and sometimes, can be misunderstood.

In this case, for example, ***a Higher Energy*** is to be shown to me.

In this instance if this were *you*, *your* Guide would be showing *you* this higher energy in a way *you* would understand. It would possibly be presented ***different***ly, in words and images that would be recognisable to *you.*

It could be presented via Jesus, Buddha, Allah, The Virgin Mary, whatever is your belief system.

Whatever your religious persuasion, all religions have one thing in common, an ultimate source, whatever form it takes.

Be it science, or whatever your own belief system is, we all have a purpose. It is for each individual to **choose** *to* find, **or not**, their particular purpose in life.

Its not about one religion over another, it's about the understanding of our being here.

This meditation is a method to illustrate more levels of understanding and **higher forms of energy**. After this next meditation (I hope), it will become apparent why I gave it this introduction.

To be quite honest, I've never thought of myself as a particularly religious person. I go to church for the usual weddings, christenings, and funerals, and I'm not very knowledgeable about the Bible, Christianity or any other religion for that matter. It only plays a small part in my life. I tend to think of myself as a pretty ordinary, 'normal' person, but I do believe there **is** something out there, other than the life we lead here on the planet, but I don't feel that I need to go to church to connect with it. This is only **my** belief, and whatever anyone else's path is, or wherever it takes them, is their choice.

The path that I am taking is opening my eyes to 'something,' but as yet I can't fully explain what it is. I do know, for sure, that it is fascinating.

My journey to the Astral Plane this time was a solo affair. I felt the need to speak to Marie-Anne again, asking to see Arthur's face, as he never appears to me clearly. I'm still so unsure of what he looks like though I have a feeling he has dark hair.

As I was writing this, I felt I was being shown some beautiful brown eyes, but the rest of his face was obscured with a mask or a cloth of some sort. I reckon they were having a right old joke up there!

I opened up using the ball cleansing Meditation, to help my body revitalise as it was tired from the exercise class that I had attended on the Friday night. I went up in the mist, out through the trapdoor, and made my way to the waterfall. On my way down to the waterfall, I still felt that there was someone besides myself there, a figure on the embankment. It's been present on the last two or three meditations. I had previously asked Sheryle if she could let me know who this figure was, or put my mind at rest as to who this Spirit could be. I felt that he or she was a very important person, so at the time of speaking to her I took a deep breath and asked if it could possibly be Jesus. She looked straight at me not answering, so I asked again with a smile.

"Was it? Is it?" I kept on. "He is there, isn't he?" I asked again. Sheryle smiled.

I had wondered if it could be Him, the first time I had sensed the figure there, but never in a million years had I ever truly thought I would be right. Anyway, when I passed the spot where I usually felt this presence, on this occasion I thought I saw something move, and then I picked up on a man with brown hair wearing a white robe.

I hurried across the stones, over to the waterfall, going on my way so as not to interfere with whatever he was doing, and started to cleanse myself under the waterfall. It was beautiful under there. I turned to cleanse my back and was facing the cave. In the middle of the cave, emerging from the darkness, I could see a blue crystal like the one I have at home. It was being lit up by a light which appeared to be coming from behind it or from within it. It was absolutely mesmerizing.

I was aware of feeling a presence beside me, a wonderful calm, gentle energy from a male with brown hair, wearing a white robe, who confirmed that the crystal was my crystal, and that it was being charged with energy so I could communicate better with my healing Guides, and that all would become clearer for me. Great! I thought. That's just what I need… and then…. realisation kicked in.

He was actually communicating with *me!* '*He*' was the important one from outside. Jesus, I thought!

Jesus! He was talking to **me**! Grace Nightingale! Now I was dreaming. I had to be!!

It looked like the Jesus image I have in my head from the Sunday school books!

This couldn't be happening...Could it?

He told me that He was pleased with how I was progressing with the healing. I was speechless. Jesus was pleased with me? I kept my head down, feeling that I was not worthy to look Him directly in the face, and also as I was feeling very shy.

He was communicating with me, but I missed it mainly because I wasn't sure if He **was** really speaking to me.

It was all a bit much to take in, and I couldn't get over the fact that He would actually want to speak to me. He was telling me that He was pleased with what I was doing, and then He put me in a bubble.

It was really thick skinned, like the skin present inside a goose egg. It made me feel that if I did a roly-poly I wouldn't hurt myself in the process. It was weird. I don't remember it having a colour, but it felt really good to be inside it.

Now I could hear Him better.

"Thank you!" I said.

Wow! Here I was speaking to 'You Know Who'. Unreal or what?

He was quite a big man, and had a fatherly air about him, an air of authority I thought. Here I was chatting to the man Himself. Then remembering Marie-Anne, I began worrying about keeping her waiting and I missed what He said next. I wondered whether I should ask Him to repeat what He had said, but I didn't like to. Whether He could tell or not what was going through my mind I don't know, but He said I should go to see Marie-Anne and that she would have something for me.

I thanked Him and went to find Marie-Anne over by the tree. I noticed in the bushes yellow and blue coloured birds resting, which Tom had also seen on previous meditations. I could see fish in the

river and things flying around, like dragonflies or even…no… fairies?
No!

Behind the bushes was a hill, and in the distance I could make out a grand building on the top. It was bathed in a white or was it gold light? It resembled a Disney castle minus the pointy roofs. It looked stunning, not so much the actual building, but the light that surrounded it.

Marie-Anne spoke then, "We have a treat for you."

Out of the blue sky there appeared a beautiful white horse, not any old white horse, but a beautiful winged, white horse. It came to rest beside me.

Oh my goodness, I thought. Whatever next?

The horse started gently shaking its head. I absolutely love horses, their smell, their shape, but unfortunately for me I'm not keen on riding them. I become very nervous at the thought of it, and I'm a little frightened of them close up.

"This is Pegasus," said Marie-Anne.

I could feel tears in my eyes at the beautiful sight before me. The whiteness of the horse was almost blinding.

"If you like, he'll take you for a ride," offered Marie-Anne.

All my nervousness surprisingly vanished. I was thrilled at the invitation. A ride or a 'fly' on a horse called Pegasus! Wow! How fantastic is that!

Then the thought of how I was going to mount the horse crept in, but before I could work myself up into a panic….. I was there! I leant down and pulled Marie-Anne up too, so she could accompany me and share the enjoyment, and as weird and unbelievable as it may seem, I even felt the warmth of the horse's body against my skin, under my legs. It was mighty strange, to say the least.

As we soared above the translucent clouds, we could see the scenery below us.

I was ecstatic, and shrieked and yelled with joy. Well, it's not everyday the opportunity arises to fly on a beautiful winged horse!

It swooped down and then climbed higher, turning one way, then another, again and again. It was fabulous! Out of this world, if you pardon the pun!

I felt as free as a bird, not frightened at all, elation running through my veins. Marie-Anne was quiet, but I felt as though she was enjoying her flight. She was smiling. I thought Arthur might have liked to join us, but then thought there is only room for two.

We could see tepees, and the beautiful castle-like building, the waterfall and the tree of knowledge.

All of these sights were spaced out like small villages, and in the distance I could see pyramids. It didn't feel as though I was to observe these today. Maybe they were for me to view on another day, another time.

As I mentioned, Pegasus had a white coat and where the wings attached, it was peculiar to see hair and feathers on the same animal. The feathers were just as white as the hair on its back. Wonderful!

We descended slowly and gracefully back to where Arthur was standing. It was the most unusual and exotic treat I think I've ever had, and I just couldn't stop smiling or thanking them all so much. I'm sure I was still floating as I made my way back to the trapdoor.

Later on in that day, I felt the energy surrounding my blue crystal in my treatment room. It made me glow all over, and the energy I felt can only be described as heavenly and much stronger now.

As for Arthur's face, it had appeared as if he was wearing a mask, a harlequin mask, and I could see only these wonderful brown eyes peering out from behind it. I was certainly being teased, wasn't I?

When I spoke to Margaret and Sheryle later, they explained the significance of the Meditation. The 'bubble' that I was put in was to enable me to hear what was being said to me, because the vibration of this soul, in the image of Jesus, is so much higher than mine, and I wouldn't have been able to hear Him properly. Margaret then went on to ask if I knew what the appearance of the winged horse meant. I hadn't a clue, and told her so.

"Well," said Sheryle, "it means that not just yet, but when you are ready, you will be working with the purest, highest, universal healing energy that there is. Its colour is magenta and there is no energy higher."

My mouth dropped open. I'm sure they must have heard it hit the floor. I was totally gob smacked! To be working with such beautiful energy would be a true privilege.

"Yes, the horse is beautiful, and the horse's tail is magical," Sheryle explained. "When it brushes against you it enables you to have an insight into all the work that healing Spirits are doing to help you, when you are using the energy to heal people."

"Oh my goodness," I gasped. Now I really can't wait to get there.

So to clarify this meditation: This was my personal journey, I did not actually meet Jesus but was shown a **Higher Energy** in the **image** of Jesus, which I recognise from my Sunday school days. At the time of this meditation, though, I did not understand this concept.

For *you* the Reader, it could be *shown to you* as Allah, Buddha, a Pope, Rabbi, or even John Wayne! It depends on what your beliefs are.

This, I feel, is one of our society's biggest failures: each interpretation that has been seen has been taken as '**The right way**', instead of the bigger picture, which is that **They Are All Correct**, presented to each person in a way that **They** understand.

JUST MARGARET AND ME

12th November 2008

THIS MEDITATION WAS THE FIRST one that Margaret and I had done on our own. Tom was feeling unwell and didn't want to pass on his bugs to Margaret, so he stayed home. I still wished to go, so drove down on my own.

We had a chat and a cuppa, then we started.

Margaret gave me a quick run through of what I was to be doing. I was to open up in the usual way and cleanse myself as always in the waterfall, after which I would meet Marie-Anne by the stream. I was instructed to look into the shallow water and observe what was there, also, to sense what it felt like, then to look deeper because Margaret had hidden something there for me to find. Margaret also told me to look on the surface of the water, and to notice what that looked like too, and generally look around and see if there was anything else going on.

It seemed a bit strange 'opening up' without Tom beside me: the room had an empty feel about it. As I arrived on the Astral Plane, I walked along the gravel path to the tree, noticing that on the plateau there was a group of people waving to me. I smiled at them then started to walk over the stepping-stones. 'The Man Himself' was still there! I cleansed myself under the waterfall, then went back out to where Marie-Anne was waiting. We made our way down to the stream, over the grass, down to the bank. I could see that the water wasn't flowing as fast as I originally thought it was, given the loud noise of the waterfall. The surface of the water, on close inspection, appeared to be a silvery colour, with the light reflecting off it, making it quite difficult to peer into, so I tiptoed in and put my face below the surface. It felt cool around my calves and hands, and almost prickly like the texture of a mohair jumper. Strange to describe water in this way, but that's the description that first came to mind.

There were plants that resembled grasses, but the leaves looked quite thick. These plants stood about four inches high and were swaying gently in the water. I saw what I thought were tadpoles and newts, and then some small neon fish that you can find in tropical water. That was really odd, having a mixture of cold and warm water creatures in the same environment. Then, thinking back to what I had experienced on my last Meditation, I came to the conclusion that absolutely anything was possible. The silt or sand under my feet felt soft, and I sensed that there were occasional flat stones there too. All in all, the sensation was a very pleasant one.

I looked at Marie-Anne and asked if I was to venture in deeper, and she gestured for me to carry on.

Pushing the light on my chest, that Marie-Anne had given me to make things brighter, I could see where I was going and was sensing more, and could feel the water around my shoulders. This, strangely, felt warmer in the deeper water than in the shallows. It also felt softer. I looked all around and spotted the same grass-looking plants that I had seen earlier in the water, only a lot bigger and moving quicker with the current. Then I thought I saw a dolphin, but logic ruled it out, which meant I was in danger of spoiling the meditation. I was doubting what I was seeing as it was only a stream.

Marie-Anne persisted with her quest to get me through this Medication, and I was back on track. I then saw a seal and a manatee, the latter is a huge sea cow, found in the warm waters of Southern America. (I've always had a secret desire to touch one of those).

As quickly as it took my brain to name it, a mermaid swam by. I got only a fleeting glance, so wasn't totally sure I had really seen one. There were all sorts of different fish, some that resembled Koi carp, a lovely deep orange and black colour, and one that was bright yellow. A goldfish darted past. I looked at the surface of the water and noticed that it was all ripples and waves, but didn't feel that the current was as strong as it first looked.

I almost forgot the task that I was to undertake! I was enjoying myself so much that I had wandered away from the task set. I remembered Margaret telling me that I had to look deeper, and try and find what she had put there for me. I concentrated hard, peering into the water again, and I thought I could see what looked like a china cup and saucer, with a blue feather or fern-like pattern painted on it, similar to the one on Margaret's cup that she was drinking from earlier in the evening. This cup, however, looked like it was made from fine bone china. It had a very delicate handle, whereas Margaret's cup was a little chunkier.

To the left of the cup, flowing down the stream, I could see a clear, ball-shaped crystal, like a tennis ball, and it was glowing. A little further down from that I could see a brass-looking thing. I wasn't too sure what object it was, but sensed that it was made of a metal of some sort. It could have been Turkish, though I'm not sure why that came to mind.

Feeling I'd completed the task that I'd been set, I decided to have a swim around. Hold on! I suddenly had an embarrassing thought: I could be skinny –dipping! I didn't know whether I had a swimming costume on or not, so I looked down at my legs, but then I wasn't sure if my legs were, in fact, a tail?

"Am I a mermaid?" I asked Marie-Anne.

"You can be whatever you like," she replied

I quite liked the idea of mermaid, so I decided to give my new flipper a try. There was no effort for me to move in the water, so I swam up to the surface and dived down, watching the light bounce off parts of the stream. It looked magical. The thought that I wouldn't be able to breathe under the water never even entered my head.

Then for some crazy reason, I had a vision of a teddy Bear sitting on the river- bank, putting his paws in the water. This then changed, and became my big, brown beautiful Bear. I wondered if he would like a swim too. I beckoned for him to join me in the water. I think I saw him with water up to his thighs, and his little tail bobbing above the water. He looked to me like he was having a ball, splashing around and then diving in and out of the water.

Margaret's voice reached me, "You have five minutes."

Marie-Anne and I laughed at my efforts to get out of the water with a huge, mermaid tail flip- flopping. Then the squelching, as I tried to walk with it up the grass, made us laugh even harder. It was certainly very awkward, there seemed to be water absolutely everywhere.

I thanked Marie-Anne and Arthur (because he is always present) for my lovely time and for their help, and made my way back down through the trapdoor. My legs were my own as soon as I had reached the path, thank goodness.

I came back into Margaret's sitting room and I opened my eyes to see her grinning at me.

"Well then, how was that?" she enquired.

I was still smiling about my mermaid experience and told her everything I had seen and felt.

The cup in the deep water turned out to be a jug made of bone china with her mug's pattern on it. She questioned about the crystal, and asked me what it did. I didn't know, so she told me to ask Marie-Anne.

"It gives light," I said.

"And".... Margaret probed.

"Energy," I replied.

"Yes," she said, "a vibration."

The other object I saw that was metallic, Margaret had been informed would be a ring, Spirit had apparently changed the shape. She laughed at my mermaid's tail and thought the animals and fish were great, including the token goldfish. When I told her about the teddy Bear, she laughed again at the thought, and explained that when things are made fun, learning takes place more easily.

My lesson for this evening, Margaret revealed, it was 'Feeling Cleansing Water Vibrations'.

I think I had done well.

Now seeing as Tom couldn't be with us that evening, Margaret asked if I was prepared to do a Meditation for him, to talk him through opening up the chakras and lead him up to the tree. She explained I would need to have to talk to Marie-Anne, just as she does with Saul, her Guide, to get all the details.

Crikey! I'm not sure whether I'm able to do this, I thought. I might mess it up or get it all wrong. I admitted my doubts to Margaret who reassured me again that

I would be fine. What I had to do was talk to Marie-Anne, and she would help me with what was needed.

I left Margaret and made my way home. The journey seemed longer this time, as there was no one to share my evening with, but I couldn't wait to get back and tell Tom what I was going to do with him.

Working with Marie-Anne

14th November 2008

I
T WAS TWO DAYS AFTER my Meditation with Margaret. I was at home and it was time for me to have my chat with Marie-Anne. I opened up in the usual way and met with Marie-Anne by the tree.

The people gathered on the plateau were waving again, so I briefly waved back and then looked over and said hello to J.C.

Hurrying along over the stepping stones across the stream, I went up the bank and behind the waterfall. I cleansed myself under the water. Turning to cleanse my back, I could see another of my crystals inside the cave. This time it was cherry quartz and didn't appear to be lit up as much as the blue one had the other day, but then as I looked closer, the blue one was present too. The red crystal had a glow within, so after cleansing, I stepped deeper into the cave for a closer look.

"We have also charged that one with energy to help you, "spoke J.C from behind me.

Oh my! He's talking to me again, I thought, but this time was aware that I couldn't feel a bubble around me as I had before, to aid communication. Maybe it was still there and I hadn't realised.

J.C explained that I was to help Tom to learn healing, and just as Marie -Anne had shown me to do it, with love as always, and always to give love to everyone and everything. He gave me a couple of instructions for my boys as well.

Then he took hold of my hand and I could feel energy being transferred into my finger around my knuckle where I had got it stuck in a bowling ball a couple of months before.

"This energy," he said, "is Magenta and what you will be using in time."

It felt different to the white light that I normally experience, it was less dense and I could see a deep red colour with lighter, small red dots, suspended within it.

I felt a cool tingle on my back between my shoulder blades, where I had been having a few niggles lately. It felt lovely: the deep red colour came to mind again, just like a red wine. It felt deeply loving. I hadn't felt anything like it before, or at least not that I had been aware of.

I thanked Him and I could see that he had shoulder length hair and lovely blue eyes. He was still dressed in His white robe and I felt extremely honoured that He had spoken to me.

It was then that I realised I could actually see His face. It was the first time I could see a face really clearly in my meditations. Yippee!!

He was showing Himself to me as a man of approximately thirty five years, with eyes very clear and a vibrant blue, which looked kindly into my eyes. His face was oval with a straight nose and strong jaw, all in good proportion, and His skin was lightly tanned with pinkish cheeks, and on his red lips a loving gentle smile put me at my ease. He had a gentle manner that made me feel nothing was too much trouble.

I made my way back to Marie-Anne who was waiting by the tree; catching sight of the gathering on the plateau for the second time. I could see my Dad, Granny, Granddad and I think I caught a glimpse of my 'second Dad' there too. I'm not sure who else was with them, as I can't always see clearly. I waved again and shouted hello. They all smiled and waved back.

Arthur was waiting with Marie-Anne, and now I could see his face properly too. It was only a brief glimpse, but he looked handsome: dark hair, brown eyes, quite young, maybe in his twenties or early thirties. He had olive skin and a beautiful smile.

I commented to Marie-Anne how lucky we were as he was quite gorgeous! She reminded me that it was I who was the lucky one, as he was my Gatekeeper. Marie-Anne's face was clearer too. Her features had changed, from a lady around my age to one who appeared a lot younger, with her beautiful young face and delicate features.

"I'm lucky to have you too," I whispered. "I love you both and thank you for making my life such a happy one."

I felt a group hug was happening: it was a whole envelopment of energy that had surrounded me that felt like unconditional love.

Back to business. Marie-Anne was to give me instructions for Tom, what I needed to do was to go back down through the green mist, and keep my chakras open, not close down. Marie- Anne would instruct me and I could write it down, just as Margaret did for us.

This is how Tom's Meditation was to proceed: Tom will open up and go to the waterfall as usual, then return to the tree with William. William will take him to the wood, in the centre of which there will be a pond that Tom is to enter. I am to tell him the water will be green and murky.

After entering the water, he is to scrutinize it to discover what is in it. The water will become clear as soon as he enters it. He is to feel the vibration of the water.

A statue of an Angel at the far end of the pond will be keeping watch. There will be fish and tadpoles in the pond, along with plants, and at the bottom of the pond will be my blue crystal, lit up. He will not be allowed to touch it, and must be told this. There will be deer drinking at the water's edge. He may or may not see these things. He is to spend fifteen minutes at this location and then return to the path and go back to the trapdoor.

Marie -Anne told me I needed to be present on the Astral Plane also, to observe Tom's actions.

I thanked everyone in Spirit I could, for giving me this opportunity and felt honoured to be given the chance to prepare a Meditation for Tom.

On this occasion, because I was leading the meditation, I feel I can relay what happened with Tom's Meditation, as it was an extension of mine.

It went as follows:

That evening we were quietly sat in our own front room, and together followed Margaret's routine of opening up the chakras and ascending to the Astral Plane. I then 'talked' Tom to the waterfall and then to the tree to meet William.

After this, I was silent.

I watched as Tom made his way with William, his Guide, to the pond in the wood. Spirit had cleared a path for him to walk along. Tom was stopped in his tracks by the appearance of a pure white deer standing a little distance away and looking straight at him. He had no idea of its significance and didn't wish to disturb it, so carried on. At the far end of the pond was my blue crystal on a bench. Hmmm! I thought. That's not quite as Marie-Anne said.

I could see Tom, William and Tainetua, Toms' Gatekeeper, standing beside the pond.

As Tom stood hesitantly waiting to enter the pond, there was an almighty shove and his Gatekeeper hurried him along and pushed him in! As he unceremoniously entered the water, to his relief, it became a clear blue.

Tom surfaced, and from where I was standing a little way from the pond, I could see him splashing around, swimming and diving. In the next instant his Gatekeeper, who was a huge Mongolian warrior, began dipping his toes in and out of the pond. He appeared to chuckle, putting his hand over his mouth, while he continued to dip his foot in and out of the water, changing feet, and chuckling.

Tainetuas' large boots were discarded beside him and his feet looked like they really needed a good wash, while his yak skins quivered as he jumped about. He looked really funny, I have to say.

That was not in the script, I muttered to myself.

William was looking at Tainetua with a slightly pompous expression or maybe it was disgust, as if to say, "Good heavens, what a way to behave!"

Tom appeared above the surface of the water once again, his fifteen minutes on the Astral Plane were up and it was time for him to leave.

"You have five minutes," I told him aloud.

I watched as he got out of the pond and walked along the path back into the green mist. Both of us returned down through the trapdoor into our sitting room. He had done well.

Tom hadn't liked the look of the murky green water so his Gatekeeper, Tainetua, had pushed him in.

Once in it, he found it was warm and it turned blue, and he could make out fish swimming. These fish apparently took on a strange appearance, and he tried to swim after them but the water seemed to plunge to a greater depth and he couldn't see clearly, so he swam back up to the surface.

What Spirit did with the crystal was brilliant. Tom was supposed to find it in the depths, but hadn't dived far enough so They placed it on the bench, and Tom spotted it.

Funnily enough, when I first cleansed my blue crystal before using it, *in real time*, I placed it in water which turned bright blue, just like the colour of the water that Tom had seen. On the Earth plane, I had found out that this particular crystal should not be submerged into water or it will dissolve, so maybe that also applies on the Astral Plane?

Tom had not seen the stone Angel that I was told he would see at the far end of the pond, but then he recalled seeing a plaque on the bench itself, and asked William to show him what was on it.

Tom smiled at the answer that he could now visualise in his mind's eye.

I wondered if it was something related to his mum, as sometimes benches have plaques dedicating them to a deceased loved one, but there was just the one word etched into the plaque in bold letters, and it read...

ANGEL!

Wow!!

We actually did it! What the significance of the white deer was we have yet to discover.

Tom's lesson from Margaret, via Marie-Anne and me was:

'A leap of Faith.'

Being confronted with the horrible green pond water, and having the faith to go into it, only to have it turn clear blue, was the central point of the Meditation. I was so proud of him, he'd done so well. We were both thrilled to bits and couldn't wait to tell Margaret.

Some of the Best Love

18th November 2008

It was four days since I had last spoken to Marie-Anne, and I really felt as if I needed to have a chat with her to get a clearer understanding of where all of this was leading, and what my path was. I guess I was feeling a bit 'lost' and didn't really know where I was going.

As I was talking to Marie-Anne, up on the Astral Plane, I could see a group of people above the waterfall, on the plateau, my dad being one of them. As I scrutinized the area, they appeared closer, almost like I had zoomed in on them. Strange. I had not felt myself move. It was inexplicable. Maybe I had drifted towards them, or my perception of them had become sharper; I don't know. Anyway, there was a whole gang of them here.

"Would you like to meet them?" Marie-Anne asked.

I certainly would!

Then, instantly appearing beside me stood my Grandparents. My Grand-dad was smiling as he always did. He was a big man with thinning hair and had tiny little round glasses. He looked just as I remembered him. He was a man with a big heart, always loving and caring. I used to sit on his lap happily as he brushed my hair, it must have been for hours at a time.

Granny, bless her heart, was a lovely person too. But my memories of her when I was a little girl were of her being quite a strict lady. They were almost like a 'good cop bad cop' team, making sure we were on the straight and narrow. As I became older; she became quite loving, or I behaved myself better, is probably more accurate! Here now, they both gave me the most wonderful hugs. It felt fantastic.

After this I saw my second dad, Philip, who scooped me up in his big arms and it felt like he had lifted me off the ground. He was a huge man, and I felt a tear of happiness to be in his company again, bless him. He had meant so much to me when I was growing up, and now I had the chance to thank him for all he had done for me over the years. If it hadn't been for him I would never have been the proud owner of my motorbike and experienced the independence that gave me. Unfortunately, the bike was forever breaking down and I was no mechanic, but I did know the size of the spark plug because it ate so many, in fact, I still remember it today! Philip was always there with a trailer to pick me up and fix it, then send me on my way again. He was such a kind and caring man. What a star! I thanked him for the tremendous support that he had given me, unconditionally, and for that I will always love him and be so grateful to him.

Then came Val. Wow! I couldn't believe it! She, also was such a truly special friend, who died under very sad circumstances. Now she was here, and gave me such a heart- warming hug that made me cry. It felt so good after all this time.

I had always been able to count on Val to be there when I was feeling sad. She could be guaranteed to put a smile on your face, anybody's face.

If I felt trapped in my life or just down in the dumps, she was always there. She never judged, she was just a pillar of support. I would always be grateful to her for giving me a sanctuary when I was in need of cheering up, and somewhere I could get over the grumps! She was still as I had remembered her: blonde hair, dark glasses, and accompanied by Barney, her beloved dog. Her dog was a scream! Whenever I visited Val, Barney would disgrace himself by mounting the cushions, and poor old Val used to get so embarrassed.

Still looking at all who were before me, I picked out our old dog, Lady. She was adorable! When Lady and I visited Val, quite often the four of us would go off for lovely long walks, often Barney couldn't quite contain his excitement and would get up to his antics. One time I can clearly remember a look of utter distaste on Lady's face as she witnessed his unruly behaviour. It was hysterical!

Lady was now standing before me, wagging her tail, or was it the tail wagging the dog? What a thrill! I bent down and got my face licked, bless her.

Cindy, our old cat from my childhood, was also here.

The family always had to be careful when stroking him, as Cindy liked only his head touched: anywhere else and he'd go for us with a nasty bite. He was always regarded as a grumpy old thing and we just left him alone. Remembering this, I decided to play it safe and just touch him on the head as I'd done in the past. Mum thought it was a female when we first got him, hence the name, and quickly it became 'too late to change it', apparently. I'm sure he had a complex about it.

It then dawned on me that there before me, appeared to be every pet from goose to guinea pig, that we had ever owned, and believe me, there had been a fair few over the years.

I now realized that between 1st October and the 18th November 2008, I had met up with all of my closest, nearest and dearest who had passed on.

This Meditation was given to me from Marie -Anne and was truly incredible in so many ways, and on so many levels. I had so much to learn! It was amazing and exciting, and I felt it would hold no bounds.

From all of my nearest and dearest I felt a huge hug of happiness now spilling over me, on the Astral Plane. It felt absolutely euphoric. I knew now I was not lost, on the contrary, I was exactly where I was supposed to be.

THE INDIAN VILLAGE

26th November 2008

THE LAST FEW WEEKS HAD flown by. Life at home carried on as normal, though I had taken some time off work because of back pain.

The house still needed cleaning and the shopping and cooking weren't going to be done by any Spirit other than myself, so it was lovely for Tom and me to 'have our escape' as it were, down at Margaret's house, back-ache and all. There was no way I was going to miss my visit, even if Tom had to carry me.

This week, Margaret explained, we were going to the Indian Village.

Reader, I must say again that this is presented to me in a way that is understandable to me. I have never visited a true Indian village, so my limited knowledge is only of the westerns on the television on a Sunday afternoon.

Those of you who have experienced the real thing and say:

"It's nothing like that." I humbly apologise to you. But this is how it was given to me.

We would be met on the bridge by two Indian braves: my Indian was a Sioux named Swishcannon, and Tom's was from another tribe. They were to escort us into the village where we were to look around and see as much as possible. We were to look closely for something that would appear 'out of place' to us.

Margaret then led us up onto the Astral Plane; we met our Guides Marie-Anne and William, and then Margaret left us by the tree as usual.

We walked on and met our Indian escorts: mine was a lot smaller than Tom's. He had short, shiny black hair with a fringe and he was of slight build and had tanned skin. On his back was a quiver full of arrows, fixed to a leather strap that lay diagonally from his shoulder to his waist. His energy felt warm and friendly. He was smiling as he led me to the right hand side of the village.

Tom's escort was dressed similarly to mine but had longer hair, and led him off to the left.

All of a sudden I was surrounded by dozens of children; they were all very loud and excitable. I was introduced to an older child who appeared to be in his teens, a young man who, I believe, could have been my Indian brave's son. He smiled and appeared to nod in acknowledgement of me. I felt myself nodding and giving him a smile in return, feeling rather delighted that Swishcannon wished me to meet his son.

I could make out women in the background, busying themselves with day- to –day chores, occasionally glancing in my direction, but seeming too shy to make eye contact.

Swishcannon led me to a tee-pee with a huge eagle painted on the outside. He pulled back the opening and gestured for me to step inside. As I entered, my first thought was that it appeared a lot bigger inside than it looked from the outside; in fact it was huge.

I glanced around the tent. To the left was a small, blue, earthenware pot or vase that caught my eye. Was this the out- of- place thing Margaret wished me to find?

I carried on scanning the inside of the tee-pee and came across what looked like spears. Thinking of the instructions that Margaret had given us, I thought that maybe the spears were the odd things out, as I didn't think they needed to hunt up here on the Astral Plane, but then Swishcannon had arrows. I didn't think they would be killing anything up here?

Logic and doubt entered my mind and I concluded that these spears were what I would **expect** to see in an Indian village, so dismissed the 'spear' idea as imagination. I scanned the other side of the tee-pee where there was an assortment of furs on the floor and then some pieces of fabric that were beautifully coloured and had beads woven within them.

A little further round the tee-pee was what looked like a raised area, which I assumed was a bed. It looked nice and warm, again with furs and fabric, all very pretty and welcoming.

In the centre of the tee-pee was a fire with stones placed around it. As I looked up, I caught a glimpse of the sky through an opening in the top. Large poles made from tree branches formed the opening of the tepee. It was impressive.

Suddenly the flap covering the opening was pushed to one side and in walked a small gentleman wearing a headdress of feathers, which were woven into an arch that framed his head, and which hung down both sides of his body to the ground. He looked very old. I assumed he was the Chief. His features were soft and his skin was very wrinkly. I felt I should bow to him out of respect and avoid direct eye contact.

We settled around the fire, sitting cross-legged opposite each other, Swishcannon to my left. They were smoking a pipe, handing it round, and I felt it pressed into my hand. The next thing I knew, I was puffing on it. But I gave up smoking years ago, I thought! The sensation of smoking seemed to open up my throat and airways, and I was convinced I was going to explode in a coughing fit any minute. This didn't happen, and I seemed to manage the pipe without embarrassment. I took three or four deep puffs and handed it to my left.

I then felt as if I was being given a drink, and looked down to see a small bowl. It looked as if it had been carved from wood. I was amazed with what I was experiencing.

The Chief then reached over and took my hands. He seemed to be examining them very closely, turning them palm up and scrutinizing them, and then he turned them over again. He bowed his head to touch my hands with his forehead. I felt extremely honoured and wondered what it all meant.

It was strange, as I felt that they were showing me that they were honoured to be meeting *me*. Was it because they knew I had done healing with my hands? I was being held in high regard even though I was a female. I smiled to myself. It was *I* who was the one who was honoured to meet them!

Suddenly I felt a huge shove to my right, as if someone had accidentally knocked into me. I looked over to see this enormous, furry, brown Bear plonk himself beside me. His massive feet were stuck out in front of him and the children were laughing and trying to snuggle up close to him, playing with him and his beautiful fur. I started to giggle, and then reminded myself that this was probably not the appropriate way to behave. He was sat on his backside like a real person, his huge feet were stuck right out and his big brown nails shone in the light that was coming in from the opening of the tent.

All at once we appeared to be moving. The chief led me out of the tee-pee and as I left the tent, straight in front of me I caught a brief glimpse of an Angel. It was translucent, like smoke, and had massive wings. It seemed to be just sitting on a fence, as far as I could tell, and it was a lovely blue-white colour and absolutely 'other worldly'.

To my left I could see animal skins that had been stretched out to dry in the sun, and in the distance I could make out buffalo and numerous dogs running around. There was so much activity going on I found it really difficult to take it all in.

A magnificent light-chestnut cavalry horse was being shown to me. It had a blaze down its nose and was quite big. The Indians presenting it to me appeared to be very proud of their animal. I wasn't sure whom it belonged to either, if it had been captured or how they had acquired it, but it was truly a handsome beast.

Next, I was presented with a leather strap, which had been made into a headband. There were two feathers positioned along it. I felt a bit disappointed that I hadn't brought a gift for them. Swishcannon was wearing a necklace made from a leather strip. There were two beads attached to it and he took it off and put it over my head for me to wear. Wow! How lovely is that? I thought. How or what could I offer in return? I had no idea, I had nothing with me.

It was time to go already. I remembered to thank my Indian escort and the Chief for all the hospitality and kindness I had been shown. I felt honoured that they had allowed me to see into their world.

Back in Margaret's sitting room we were praised for our efforts. She told me that the buffalo was her power animal and the Bear was mine. Tom's was a wolf. I remember seeing lots of dogs but don't remember if I saw a wolf or not. The children I had seen with my Bear were Margaret's Spirit children, as well as the Indian children. The blue vase was to do with healing, as was to do with the chief being interested in my hands.

Both Tom and I saw the eagles on the outside of our tee-pees; Tom's also had a deer or antelope painted on his. There had been many other tee-pees but they looked fairly plain.

The only thing I missed was a shepherd's crook, which was situated inside the tee-pee, which I could have easily dismissed along with the spears I had seen. Margaret went on to explain that apparently, they did have spears, arrows etc and all the trappings that native Indians had, otherwise they would look the same as the rest of us. The implements weren't used for hunting, only for us to find on our Meditation. They were put there by Margaret's Guides this time, not by Margaret. The shepherd's crook had been the object that was out of place, as the Indians didn't have sheep.

Margaret's Guides are members of Jesus' disciples and of course... 'part of his flock'. It was their joke. Very clever!

As for giving gifts, Margaret told us that all we had to do was *think* of what we wanted to give as a gift, and it would appear. How wonderful! I will remember that for next time.

Also this evening, we were to undertake some healing with Margaret. She showed us how to scan the body and explained to us how to see the different colours that the body has. Tom found this quite easy as he can see auras; I did think I was going to be a bit slow to pick it up, as I don't see aura colours, but 'feel' them. I used my hands to scan down Tom's body but found it difficult to 'see', although I 'felt' the colours should be greens, reds and oranges. I couldn't really say whether I was 'seeing' the colours in my mind's eye, but more what I felt the colours should have been. This is how it comes for me: I feel the colours, and then I see them. The vibration can't lie; it always tells the truth so long as you know what it means, but what you **see** can be misinterpreted.

"Don't worry," Margaret said kindly, "they will come."

"I think I need more practice at it," I jokingly replied, but secretly felt a bit of a failure.

On the way home Tom told me I should have said what I felt.

His reasoning was that once I had pronounced the colour that I'd felt, that colour would appear, and then I would see it in my mind's eye.

"Yes, that's all very well," I told him, "but I felt that it would be cheating, because I wasn't actually seeing the colour and Margaret told me to say what I see." I thought about what Tom had said and decided to take his advice and try it a bit differently next time, and see how I got on.

Our homework for this week was to practise colour scanning each other's bodies, as Margaret had shown us.

Just Wow!

BOTH TOM AND I DECIDED it was time to tackle the homework Margaret had given us from our previous visit. We started by opening up in our normal way. Tom was sitting on the sofa and when he had finished opening up, he told me his Gatekeeper had taken a bit of a fancy to my slippers that look a little like moccasin boots, and could he wear them? I told him no, because he is rather a large gentleman and I just felt that he might stretch them with his big feet.

It was all quite entertaining. We had come to realize over the last few months that Toms' Gatekeeper, Tainetua, had a real sense of humour. I left my slippers, with the toes facing inwards, abandoned in front of the sofa, just as we were about to start.

Tom was first to attempt the scanning. I sat on a chair and he started at the top of my head. He positioned one hand in front of me and the other one behind. He then stood at my right- hand side.

Apparently, as Tom was moving his hands down over my body, not touching any part of me, he could see all the colours of the rainbow coming out from under his hands. It all sounded fascinating and he said that it looked wonderful.

And it got me thinking. Did it look like a kind of Jacob's Technicolor dream coat that he could see? I wonder if *that's* what everyone had seen all those hundreds of years ago in the bible! Maybe it had been aura colours. Who knows?

Anyway, Tom continued scanning down my legs with his hands. He paused, with a thoughtful look, and then continued, scanning the other side of my body, starting at my head.

When he found the spot on my back which had been hurting, he brought in some beautiful energy. I could feel it gently pulling to the left, then to the right. It ached, then the ache moved and tingled, and fuzzed, then the pain and discomfort eased, leaving the area very pleasant. 'Glowing nicely', sprang to mind.

Tom managed to drag the painful feeling from the area where it had started, down through my legs, out of my feet! It was an amazing feeling, as I've not had very much healing done on my own body, so it was a real pleasure to receive.

"I saw the bones, the skeleton, and brought white energy in," Tom announced.

He was clearly chuffed.

"I felt I needed to make it all white, and asked up to William in my head, to make the unwell bits look grey, so I could see where I needed to bring healing in. As I finished asking, I could see all the areas that were grey. Wow!" Tom exclaimed in excitement.

"You saw it white?" I asked.

Tom was so excited I felt I needed to make sure I was hearing him ok, he was chattering nineteen to the dozen, desperate to get out his findings, bless him.

"Yes!" he affirmed. "All you have to do is ask for the bones etc. to be a white colour, and for the areas that need healing to be given a grey colour, then you can 'see' where you need to bring healing energy in."

He was so clever! I got very excited, and then realized I wasn't the one who could see the colours, Tom was! Doubt and disappointment started to creep into my thoughts: I started questioning my own ability to accomplish this task.

Then it was my turn. I scanned, or tried to scan.

Tom started giving me instructions after instructions, but I couldn't see a damn thing!

He kept on saying, "Say what you feel. Say what you feel. I was trying to tune in. After the sixth time I was ready to tell him to shut up. I could just *not* concentrate with him keeping on like that.

I tried again and this time said out loud, as I was scanning him,

"Ok! I feel white, gold, pink and blue stripes down your head!" I shouted the colours that I thought I felt, because that's how I work, with the vibration of how things feel. And as my hands moved down his body, the colours started changing. "Wow! It's working!" I realised I could now actually 'see' the colours in my mind's eye. They were like stripes. His shoulders were different colours. I saw blue for his left and gold for his right. I knelt down to scan the front and back of his body. I saw green and purple, orange and so on. His legs were orange, his knees were red and his shins were green with pink blobs and his feet were blue. Don't ask me!........ That's what I saw! The other side of his body was blue and green and all the colours of the rainbow down to his legs and his feet. Wow!

"Ask them to turn it white and for the injured bits to become grey," Tom instructed, so this I did.

Oh my! Everything was now white and I could see a grey patch on his right elbow, also on his thoracic area and on his lumber region.

"Yes that's right!" Tom confirmed, when I told him of my findings. I concentrated white healing energy into the thoracic area, which quickly turned into a deep red. Tom noticed the different feel of the energy and said it felt comfortable. After a few minutes he reported that he felt good; he had a little wiggle and said his back felt perfect. I moved on to the lower lumber area, placing my hands against the

L5 and pelvic areas, bringing in white light, which again changed to a deep red.

Then all of a sudden I could see a square block of pink. I really wasn't sure what I was being shown. It looked kind of fibrous, like a layer of bone, not a cross section but like the outside, smooth layer wasn't there. A moment later I realised that I was actually being shown inside of the sacral area of bone that looked honeycombed. The energy felt prickly, similar to the sensation that I had felt on a previous meditation, when I had put my hands in the shallows of the stream on the Astral Plane.

"Ooh, hang on a minute, that's starting to ache," said Tom

"Just you hang on a minute," I replied impatiently. I knew I had more to do, I replaced my hands. I felt I was on a roll and didn't want him interrupting. The energy started to change to a soft warm feel; I was now reminded of the energy felt in the deep water of the meditation.

Was Spirit with the healing energy washing out the bone? Washing away the pink colour? Or washing away Toms ache? I wasn't sure but Tom said it felt better, and shuffled in his seat with a big grin. I tried his elbow and could feel the pulling and pushing of the energy that was coming through, it felt quite gentle but firm.

"I can really feel that," Tom told me.

It stayed for a few moments, then started to subside and began to flow down his arm and out of his hands.

I was so thrilled. I wanted another go, and started again at Tom's head, placing one hand in front and one behind his ears, as he had done to me. Closing my eyes and concentrating, what was this I was now seeing? Not colours but a sort of shape. It was round and had a soft bumpy surface, creamy colour with a rubbery texture, and appeared to be in a shell.

Not at all sure of what I was seeing, I opened my eyes, took a deep breath, and tried to figure out the image I was being shown. Wow! Its his brain! . Eager to discover the next body part I might see, I started to move my hands down his neck and could see what looked like a fish bone. It looked a bit odd; I didn't think what I was seeing was right. Surely I should see vertebra? But…. hang on, is it vertebrae that I'm now being shown? It wasn't clear. I removed my hands and started again, this time thinking vertebrae. I saw the brain again and then vertebrae.

The bit that I could not work out looked a little like this but a creamy white colour.

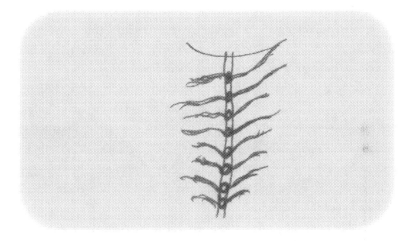

As I was scanning his body down, from his neck towards his shoulders, I saw two red veins on either side of the vertebrae… Wow! And then there was muscle, blue and red in colour across the trapezius muscle, then shoulder joint and bone and his scapula. Wow! Unbelievable! My eyes (or my brain, however you want to attribute it), couldn't comprehend what I was looking at and then, still in disbelief, I glanced over and saw two lungs!

"Tom, I've got your lungs!" I screamed with delight.

"Can you see them moving?" Tom asked.

I waited, almost holding my breath and… yes! There they were, moving as they inflated and deflated, taking air in and out of Tom's body. I moved my hands again and could see the heart muscle pumping away. It was showing a healthy red colour, thank goodness. I could pick out the diaphragm lying underneath his rib cage, and what I thought might have been his spleen, and loads and loads, well, yards of white, almost translucent intestines, quite lumpy in places, full of undigested food. Well, it wasn't long since we'd had our tea. I quickly moved on to Tom's left side and rested my hands over the front and back of his body where his lungs were. They were showing a healthy pink colour, and this time I could see the whole of his heart. It was so weird! It was like wherever I moved my hands; I could see what was between them, not below or above, just the immediate area where my hands hovered. I guess I was only to see one area at a time of what was between them. It was absolutely incredible.

Wanting to see more, I moved my hands over and picked up on Tom's liver, and two kidneys and two other small circular things, but I was so excited about it all that I couldn't even think what these circular bits might be. Maybe they were adrenal glands? Who knows? I scanned over Tom's intestines again. They appeared to be all lovely and warm and soft looking; I felt as if I could touch them. Hey! Maybe I could feel them?

"Ooh!" Tom suddenly spoke. "That feels like you're touching the inside of my stomach!"

Oh dear, I thought, maybe I shouldn't do that.....

"Oh, does it dear?" I replied.

All innocent, and trying hard to suppress a laugh.

"Yes," he replied. "That's really weird, Grace."

Best leave that area alone for the time being, I thought, and decided to move my hands up to the front of his face. I could see his eyeballs, and the inside of his mouth and nose. I moved my hands back down and saw his hip and the ball and socket joint that sits there and… oh!…I could even see which side Tom was 'dressed'… to the left!

I told him this and he quickly covered his groin with his hands, like that would make a difference! By this time, we were making so much noise laughing, and joking about our findings, we didn't stop to wonder what our Guides would be thinking of us. They probably thought we were having a riot!

My hands moved on downwards, exploring the muscles and bones in his legs until I reached his feet.

Wow! Wow! Wow! This was just too much to take on board. Margaret had only been teaching us since September. She truly is a fantastic teacher, and for us to have learnt all we have in that short space of time can only be described as amazing. Both Tom and I had Cheshire cat grins.

"I suppose you're going to tell Margaret that yours was in colour?" Tom teased, sarcastically, but with a grin.

"Oh yes," I replied triumphantly. "Yours was just white and grey wasn't it?!"

We made tea and sat down in the sitting room to talk about our findings. We were chatting nineteen to the dozen, laughing and sharing our experiences, discussing how well our homework had gone, when I suddenly looked over to where my slippers had been before we started, and noticed that they had been moved. How peculiar. There they were, on the floor with the toes pointing outwards, the heels inward, and about a foot and a half apart. It took me a moment, and then I realized.....their new position was in front of the spot on the sofa where Tom's Gatekeeper, Thainetua, would have been sat, right next to Tom. The slippers were positioned as if the Gatekeeper had been wearing them!

Tom and I couldn't stop laughing; he promised he hadn't moved them and certainly I didn't!!

"Oh my goodness, he's been wearing me flaming' slippers!" I roared to Tom, who was still holding his sides with laughter.

Now the evening had gone extremely well, but I feel I ought to be honest and mention that there was one small problem with our homework. Tom had the most overpowering wind all night. Not just the odd parp, but more like a bugle or a trumpet fanfare and the smell was obnoxious. I was sat next to the gas fire as it was the middle of winter, and I did at one point think that it was probably not the best choice of places as he might blow the whole house up.

If there was physical proof of what we had achieved during the evening, then this had got to be it. It wasn't something that you could touch but you could definitely hear and smell it. Tom's protests that I had caused it fell on deaf ears, of course. But funnily enough, when I rang Margaret to tell her, she confirmed that it was, certainly, my doing.

"Well Grace," she laughed, "you did massage his intestines!"

The 'fish bones' that I thought I had seen in Tom, I later realized, were his spinal cord and nerves in his neck.

Nothing more to say, except............"WOW"

Presents

THIS WEEK MARGARET HAD INFORMED us we would be visiting the Indian village again, and that we were to be given symbolic presents. This meditation was an important one for me, as Margaret had informed me that someone was taking my energy. The present I was to be given was to protect me, as apparently I was in need of it.

I had an inkling of who it could be but wasn't a hundred percent sure. The person I was thinking of is also in alternative therapy, and I wasn't really sure if this person was aware of what she was doing, as it is possible to drain energy from another and not know that you are doing it. Anyway, if this isn't the case, and this person is consciously aware of what they are doing, then this needs to be guarded against, Big Time! We opened up, and Margaret took us through our Meditation up onto the Astral Plane and to meet our Guides next to the tree of knowledge. I greeted Marie-Anne with a hug. When I looked around there appeared to be quite a number of people about. I wasn't sure who they all were but presumed they were all friends and relations of Tom and me.

We made our way over to the bridge and my Indian Guide, Swishcannon, greeted me.

I spied the Angel with those huge wings, sitting on the fence again, but I still didn't see the face. I asked Marie-Anne for his name and I think I caught 'Gabriel', but it wasn't very clear. He looked magnificent, translucent like blue and white smoke. I'm convinced that his wings were incredibly strong as they were so big, but because I can't see the face, I'm unsure if it's male or female.

We were escorted to the same tee-pees as last time, mine with an eagle on the outside. Once again, there seemed to be a whole big group of us. This time I caught sight of the blue vase, and looking at the spears I could see the shepherd's crook that was on the other side of them. We sat ourselves by the fire, which was unlit; well I guessed it was, as I couldn't see flames coming from it this time. Swishcannon and his family were here; I'm not sure if the chief was already here or if he followed me in.

I was given some berries and nuts to eat and then some fish. I was told we would be going on a trip down a lane. All of a sudden we were there. Just like that! There were bushes on either side.

"This is where we collect our berries,"Swishcannon said.

I wasn't sure if I heard correctly but that is what I understood. We made our way up the path.

"And nuts!" I heard someone add, as we passed even more bushes and trees. The path seemed to open out onto a plateau above the most beautiful landscape, and situated below I could see trees and hills. It looked all green and lush. Eagles were flying in the distance and I felt like I could fly with them. There was a fire with smoke bellowing from it. The Indians were showing me how to make smoke with a blanket. It looked so real I could almost smell the smoke.

We were sitting back from the edge of the plateau, and could see the splendid view below us. There seemed to be a big party of us here, including my Bear with the children all enjoying his company. It was just like a picnic.

I had been given a shawl to put around my shoulders. Then I was given what I thought was a crystal or something bright and shiny with light emitting from it. I also picked up on a leather strap of some kind, tied in a certain way to form a symbol.

It was time to move on and we were travelling on horseback. I was sat on the same light brown horse with a white blaze, that they showed me the last time I came. I also had a feeling that it was a cavalry horse once belonging to a soldier, but who, I had no idea.

Off we went, just the three of us; Marie-Anne, Swishcannon and I. Swishcannon led us to a river.

"This is where we fish," he explained. Peace and calm reigned everywhere. I could hear the birds and the gentle ripple of the river. The trees looked dense green and very fresh, and I had a definite sense of being down in the valley from where we had been situated a few moments before. It was strange. I had no feeling of getting here; no sense of the short trip I had just undertaken.

I could see Swishcannon in the water on his horse, the end of its tail gently drifting with the currant downstream. The scene was one of beauty and tranquillity.

We were moving off again, only this time going up a really steep path. My horse's head was bobbing up and down and his mane flowing with the movement of climbing such a steep path. It seemed to be a real effort and I could hear the horses' hooves stumbling on loose ground and hoped we would not tumble; I held on tight. We arrived on another plateau and it looked a little different, with what appeared to be a huge rock positioned at the back to form a smooth rock face, resembling a massive pebble.

It looked out onto another landscape, large flat grasslands stretched as far as the eye could see. Buffalo herds were peacefully grazing in the distance.

An all too familiar voice broke the silence, "Five minutes. Make sure you thank your Guides," reminded Margaret.

I was miles away!

I thanked Marie-Anne and then realised Margaret meant all of our Guides, including our Indian ones. It dawned on me that Swishcannon was also one of my Guides. I decided to thank them all just to make sure and then to thank the Chief as well. I asked Marie-Anne his name.

"Chief Sitting Bull," came her reply.

I was in awe.

"Thank you Chief Sitting Bull," I gulped, and then the next thing I knew we were right back in the village again.

I thought about the presents and the fact that I actually hadn't given Swishcannon anything. The crystal I was wearing around my neck was an amethyst and I thought that my Indian Guide might like this as a gift from me, so I symbolically took it off and gave it to him. He appeared to be pleased with the offering and I decided to give the children a football for them to have fun with. As we said goodbye I could see them all kicking it around and chasing each other. It was a pleasing sight and I felt that I had said my 'thank you' properly now.

Margaret was pleased, and with a smile asked how we had got on. Tom retold his meditation first. His experience was similar to mine with a trip out, as well. Margaret enquired if anyone got the Chief's name?

"Yes I did!" I burst out.

Tom and Margaret both tuned in and asked their Guides.

"Sitting Bull!" I excitedly revealed.

"Sitting Bull," came both their replies.

Margaret explained to me that the present given to me by the Indians was symbolic: that which I had thought was a crystal was in fact a tiny silver book on a leather necklace. On this was the symbol. It was a symbol that I had seen before but I didn't know where. The light that I had seen was the reflection shining off the silver book.

"It's Indian karma," Margaret explained.

"In the future, when you see the person who is taking your energy, all you have to do is imagine your necklace, touch the symbol on the necklace, and your protection is there."

On my previous visit to Margaret, when I had first met Sitting Bull, she had asked me when I returned from the Astral Plane, the colour of the Chief's eyes. I hadn't known because I hadn't dared look him straight in the face. But this time I looked at his eyes, and I knew the colour when she repeated the question,

"Greeny-grey," I replied. Margaret smiled and nodded.

A Trip to Maiden Castle

I THOUGHT I WOULD ADD THIS experience to my journals to share with you. I would like to say this is *not* a meditation, in the form we have been enjoying with Margaret. It's an experience that Tom and I had, while we were out for the day.

William, Tom's Guide, decided it was time for an exercise in picking up vibration when we were out and about.

During the following event, Tom and I chatted to each other, and at the same time to our Guides, so I do hope this is not too confusing as to who's talking to whom. We found it good fun and quite amazing. It 'blew me away', on the day.

Our knowledge and our awareness are continually growing with all the meditations and the different healing vibrations, along with the methods we are learning from Margaret. It is surprising what you start to pick up on. Before, I hadn't a clue how to acquire all this information.

Tom had decided to take me out to visit Maiden Castle which is the remains of an old Iron Age fort and is the biggest in Europe. It is situated just outside Dorchester in Dorset.

As we arrived I was surprised and amazed at how extensive it is: believe it or not, it's the size of 50 football pitches. All that is left today is a hill that just dwarfs you as you step out of the car; also on the top of the hill are the remains of a Roman Temple.

Now to my knowledge, I have never visited it before, but did check with my mother who didn't have any recollection of any of us going to visit it as children.

Nestled in the beautiful Dorset countryside, Maiden Castle is situated on ground surrounded by a fairly flat landscape. When we climbed to the top, the view could be appreciated in all directions for miles, and is absolutely breath taking.

Tom and I walked along the path to what would have been the main entrance. As we approached the entrance, there were two paths from which it was possible to enter. Before we were to go through the gates at the top, both Tom and I 'felt' that we were going to be taken on a 'Guided' tour of the ramparts around the huge mound.

"This way my lady," I heard William saying, to me.

Well, I thought to myself, I don't normally hear him, and I felt highly honoured. William led us around the highest mound that encircled this wonderful place, which had all been dug before man had invented the JCB!

As we walked, we were being given information about what it was like when William was here. It had been taken over by the Romans at one point; there obviously was a lot of history to this place.

In my mind's eye, I could see William standing proud in his Cathar Knights armour, over which he wore a white tunic with a red cross on it. He looked very smart.

We walked to the right of the main entrance, on the highest rampart leading off anti-clockwise around the Fort.

William gestured towards the grass on the huge banks, and explained to us that it was cut and used to feed the livestock. In my mind's eye I could 'see' small round huts that soldiers would have used, made of small woven Hazel branches and thatch for the roves.

To the west is a distant hill, which is now Thomas Hardy's Monument. In old times it was used to warn Maiden Castle of impending danger or invasion from that direction, and a fire would have been was lit as a warning, William explained.

As we continued to walk further round, the vibration of the area became much more relaxed, less rigid. The south side position was where the families would have had their living quarters.

In my mind's eye I could 'see and hear' the day-to-day goings-on and the general noise of families going about their daily business. Here had been a community working together to grow crops, tend their animals and mind their children. It was a peaceful scene with people working hard in fields in the valley below.

This day when we visited was a cold day, with a cruel wind that chilled both Tom and me. But as we continued our tour, (and again in my mind's eye), it 'felt' it could be summer, and I was in an earlier time, in the same place, wearing a long white dress and had long blonde hair. This was strange!

"This way, my lady," William gestured with his hand.

I don't know how to explain this, but as we walked around, people who were walking their dogs *in our time,* moved off the path to let us through. To them we were no one special, it was only Tom and I, and I was surprised.

But that's what happened and I have no explanation. Perhaps I imagined it?

Tom's Gatekeeper, Tainetua, laughed at a dog we saw. It resembled a large skunk and did look rather comical. Tainetua is huge, and sensing that William was feeling the cold, because they were' in our time,' lent him one of his own enormous yak skins. It really was freezing!

Arthur, my Gatekeeper, was also here with us, presenting himself as a young boy. From what we could pick up, he had not lived at the castle at the same time as William.

Marie-Anne was wearing a lovely warm cloak with a big hood, looking like she had just stepped out of a Scottish Widows television advert. She appeared to be taking interest in the beautiful landscape and where William used to live and work.

We continued walking along the ramparts and further along I could see in my mind' eye, there was a trading post, consisting of huts for people who were passing through the Fort, trading their goods, much like today's street markets.

Walking on, we quickly arrived at the entrance to the east side. This, we felt, was for things to be brought into the castle safely. The crops and provisions were brought through this entrance. As I stood in the middle of the entrance I sensed it could also have been a place for medicine and herbs to change hands. It felt as if there was a hustle and bustle of events happening all around us and I thought I should move to the side to make room -but it was only Tom and me here, in real time.

We walked on and William, now standing almost on guard, ushered us along as we approached the north side, which I concluded was the face that the enemy saw as it approached. It was massive, a foreboding range of colossal grassy mounds, each hiding dips and deep crevices. When attempting to climb up to the top, the enemy would have been met with yet another huge drop down the other side, and another enormous grass wall to climb.

We carried on walking along the highest rampart which was next to the top of the hill. Here we could stop and could enjoy the view for miles and miles around. But up here the wind blew relentlessly, it was freezing, so I was thankful for the warm clothes I was wearing.

All of a sudden a huge wave of emotion washed over me, reducing me to tears. We were meant to have come here, to walk this path around the castle and to climb the mound with William as our Guide.

Why?

Was he was actually taking me home....?

YES.

I felt there was a fanfare waiting for me. When we reached the entrance I could feel the excitement of the occupants who lived here, anticipating the arrival of someone special who was visiting, only this special someone was.... Me. I could hear the people cheering and waving saying, "She's coming, she's nearly here now."

Two flags were flying at the entrance, one red and one white, not square flags but triangular ones.

We walked towards the left entrance and saw a style and a kissing gate. As we approached, some people who were coming out, *in real time*, stepped aside once more to let us enter, just as the other people had done earlier.

"You're special" Tom said.

That's exactly how I felt – Special!

"Thank you," I said, and the strangers smiled and I nodded.

As we entered the main area of Maiden Castle, on top of the hill, I could see a huge gathering of Spirits watching us walk into their world, all with a welcoming smile, as if they had been expecting us.

"My lady," I kept hearing. But who am I, who was I? We walked down the centre of the plateau and Tom told me:

"This is where **your** house was," and he pointed to the left hand side of the path.

Only a flat grass top remains at Maiden Castle today.

"Ooh! What sort of house?" I asked him.

"Yours was one of the important families because your father was a medicine man, a healer, he healed people with his hands and was held in very high regard by members of the community. For the daughter of such an important man to return to the fold, is indeed a very special day, and given the fact that you, too, have grown and developed your healing skills, makes you a very important person in your own right. The fact that you have returned with your skills makes them **very** proud of you, and you are a part of their history and community."

Oh, Golly! I thought to myself, and felt deeply honoured that they thought of me in that way.

We wandered off from the main path towards the area where the hut would have stood. But I had a very strong feeling that maybe I should rejoin the path, as I sensed it was the proper thing to do. It was as if there were people lined along the path waiting to catch a glimpse of me. Tom said he felt like a guard, and part of my entourage to ensure a safe passage on my trip, and felt privileged to be part of the escort. He also felt that he should be respectful and not do or say anything improper towards me.

As we walked down the centre of Maiden Castle, we were struck by its vastness. About three quarters of the way down I felt I had to stop. In this area there are the remains of a Roman temple. I knew I had to visit it, curiosity had got the better of me, as we had read about the temple but hadn't been too sure where it was.

It wasn't at all how I had imagined: it was small and only the footings and small areas of the walls remain. Beside it, are the remains of a little cottage that would have been home to whoever had maintained or worked in the temple.

I could hear people cheering and welcoming us.

"My Lady," William spoke again.

He gestured towards the temple ruins.

I couldn't help smiling, looking up, but not able to see clearly now, for some reason, the people around us. But I could still hear and feel a crowd as I walked towards the temple.

On entering the temple everything became quiet, as if I had entered a building, but *in real time* there are only the remainders of the footings left. Inside the remains there is a corridor that encircles what appeared to be a small main room. I could almost sense the roof above my head and the warmth of the still air inside, in comparison to the blowing wind outside.

I walked anti-clockwise around the corridor and entered the main room. I sensed there had been an altar at the back wall, with a small and beautiful cloth spread on it on which stood a goblet, a candle and a box about four inches long. The latter was made of wood, and engraved with metal inlay.

At this point, I no longer felt that I had worked in the temple, as I had thought earlier. I was more like a visitor, and not the inhabitant; it was not a familiar feel. We then visited the cottage next to the temple, which confirmed for me that I had only ever been a visitor here.

In the Cottage there were two small rooms; the ruins were only knee high walls, which were quite thick and very well built.

We did think that one room was for living and the other for sleeping, but this was not something we were really sure about.

Tom and I sat on the wall for a rest and a chocolate biscuit, and it suddenly struck me that if they, the Spirits, could see us in *their* time, we would be sitting **in** the actual wall of the cottage. Bizarre!

So, when we had strayed from the main path earlier, to look at where my home would have been, we could possibly have walked **through** some of their dwellings. I do think that's why I had such a strong urge to stick to the path and not wander from it. How rude to walk through someone's house!

As we were sat on the wall of the cottage, we could not work out where the door would have been. We finished our chocolate break and made our exit out over the wall we had been sitting on. I had a distinct feeling that we had caused some amusement amongst the crowd as I could 'hear' giggling, which was probably because we had not used their door!

I had needed a rest and a chocolate biscuit to bring my energy back. After that I had heard and seen things more clearly. Thank goodness for chocolate!

It was time for us to leave. We had had such a fantastic time here at Maiden Castle, and I felt a touch of sadness on going so soon, but we had other things planned for our day and needed to make tracks.

We thanked everyone present for their kind, welcoming hospitality. It had been an amazing experience.

We left the Castle by the steep steps on the north side. Looking down, I was so surprised to see my black coat that it made me jump and I nearly fell down the steps: it was not the white robe I had imagined myself to be wearing.

Glancing back over my shoulder, I could see the people smiling and waving, the flags still fluttering in the warm breeze of their sunny day.

I felt a tear that I had to leave and say good-bye, but I knew in my heart that I would be back to visit, and made a promise to myself that I would indeed return on another day and stay longer.

The car park looked really small from the top of the banks, and when we finally reached the car it was with such a strange feeling: my title had been taken from me and I was once again just Grace Nightingale.

Tom drove out onto the small road. What I presumed to be a cattle grid on the way in, because I wasn't paying close attention, was just a bumpy section of road. In retrospect, Tom and I had entered a 'bubble' on our way in, and then on our way out it felt as if we had emerged from it. This bubble was like a protective area all around the castle. Of course, there would have been one, wouldn't there?!

We have since found out that William was a Cathar knight, a very important faith. They didn't believe in rich architecture or the power of the church, rather that God's temple resided within the heart. William had total indifference to material possessions and believed that God could be reached through one's own heart so there was no need for priests, rabbis or the whole hierarchy of religious institutions. In the 12th century the Cathars became very popular with rich and poor alike, as they saw all men as equals and were tolerant to other creeds and were of a very gentle faith.

The Roman Catholic Church saw them as a threat, and had the remaining knights executed by burning, in southern France. Places like Monsegùr, Rennes and Marseille in France, are the only places that show any remains of the faith today, which I find quite sad.

A Christmas Visit

CHRISTMAS HAD BEEN AND GONE, leaving me feeling a bit tired. Marie- Anne suggested a ball cleansing to clear all my chakras.

I opened up in the usual way, and sent down a green ball, which turned into a rainbow that split into seven balls, and did all of my chakras at the same time.

Well, I hadn't been expecting anything like that, I can tell you! Another colour, a deep indigo blue, completely filled my body with a huge beam. It felt like it had opened up and emptied out all the 'stodge' that had built up.

I asked if it could also clear my head, as I was experiencing a difficulty in concentrating, just as if all my knowledge and information was in a pile of books thrown in the middle of my brain, instead of neatly stacked away on shelves for easy access.

I needed help to file it all in its rightful places, so as to absorb more of the same. Gradually a grey cloud lifted, leaving me feeling as bright as a button with a clear and switched-on brain.

A beam of beautiful white light filled me up. The light changed to a magenta colour and, to put the icing on the cake, a beautiful gold egg encased my whole body.

Next it was up to the Astral Plane. J.C was beside the waterfall. I wished Him a Happy Birthday and made my way over the stepping-stones to the waterfall where I turned my back and looked into the cave. I could see a gold chest in the centre that was surrounded by light.

I heard a voice whisper, "We have gifts for you."

J.C. was beside me. He opened the chest and a brilliant, blinding gold light shone from within. He reached inside and lifted out a golden lion. It was exquisite! Standing about four inches high and between ten and twelve inches long, it shone like nothing I had ever seen before.

"It is for you," He said.

He handed it to me and as I reached out to grasp it......my chest absorbed it! I instantly felt its magnificence spread through me like a wave of warm sunshine. It tingled and fuzzed and sort of pulsated a couple of times, which took me aback.

The lion, J.C explained, was to give me the courage to stand up and build my business. I'm not good at shouting about what I do, and I think that this stems from some childhood insecurities. We had been taught that self-praise is no form of recommendation. That's how I've always lived my life, and now I've realised I need to be a little more assertive.

He took out a stick next, that magically seemed to be longer than the chest from which it came.

He attached an orb, which resembled a water droplet, to the end of the stick and told me that I could call upon this staff to produce white Energy when I needed it.

He placed a butterfly in my hair. It had big wings and was pink. He told me it was to help me feel free from the earthly ties that are sometimes overwhelming and make me feel trapped.

Next came a Tinkerbelle- type fairy,she had wings, a beautiful wand, very dainty legs and feet and she flew and fluttered around, coming to rest on my shoulder.

"This fairy is to help you bring a little magic into people's lives," He quietly declared.

"Thank you so very much," I gasped. Well, what can you say when Jesus (at least that's who *I* think it was) gives you presents on his birthday, albeit a couple of days difference.

I didn't think I had the means to reciprocate, then it occurred to me that I could give him all my love, knowing full well He would be happy with the love I could give him, and a huge hug to go with it.

I did wonder if it was the 'done thing' to go up into the Spirit world and hug Jesus.

I felt Jesus accepted the love I gave him, then gave some back, so I could pass it on to others who may be in need of it another time. Bless him.

I gave my thanks again and went to find Marie-Anne.

I felt I was full of butterflies and resembled something out of a child's fairy-tale book.

Marie-Anne was waiting for me by the tree with what seemed like quite a crowd, although I couldn't see all of them clearly. She said that there were some old friends for me to meet.

Two dark haired gents stepped forward. I instantly recognised both of them and honestly couldn't believe my eyes.

There before me, on my right, was a dear old friend who went by the name of 'Bumpy' Harcombe. I used to work alongside him. He was a dear old soul. He was short in stature with rosy cheeks because he worked in the freezers.

He was a lovely 'no-nonsense' type of man whom I dearly loved. He was such a genuine chap and always very polite and ready to help. As long as you treated him right, he would be there for you always, now here he was walking towards me and smiling.

To the left stood another wonderful surprise, a dear old friend whom I grew up with. Laurence was confined to a wheelchair and had a fantastic sense of humour.

I have fond memories of sharing some funny moments with him and the other kids of our age. Now I saw him walking, although with a kind of rolling motion similar to the way my dad had walked before having his hip operation. It was just amazing to see him, walking and pain –free.

Laurence and 'Bumpy' then gave me the most beautiful hug together. I was overcome by a huge green wave. It was so overpowering it brought tears to my eyes, seeing these special people and feeling the abundance of love we felt for each other. A magnificent and totally unexpected experience I'll always treasure.

'Bumpy departed this world suddenly. He had been out on his motorbike when he had apparently collapsed and died. It had come as a huge shock as he was only in his late thirties, early forties. It wasn't until a year after his death that I was made aware of his passing.

Laurence and 'Bumpy' knew each other and Laurence had ridden a specially designed trike, (a three wheeled motorbike) that his wheelchair fitted in. They had both belonged to the same biker group which I had seen at a race circuit one year, so it didn't surprise me to see that they had met up once again, but this time on a different level.

I knew about Laurence's passing, his funeral was just wonderful, if a funeral can be classed as that. He had one heaven of a send off, and one that did him proud. His funeral had been held on the top of the Netherminster downs at the beautiful picnic area. The vicar himself turned up on a motorbike and sidecar, robes flapping in the wind, and his passenger in the sidecar being none other than Laurence in his coffin! It was a hilarious sight which brought a smile to almost everyone's face. I don't know how he managed it, but half way through the service, the red arrows did a (totally unexpected) timely fly-over which certainly brought a lump to my throat. He was an inspiration to us all and deserved no less.

Looking back, I feel privileged to have had such wonderful friends whom I was sad to lose but was happy to find again up here! Who needs presents at Christmas when the universe can give you things money just can't buy?

OUR VISIT TO BADBURY RINGS

IT WAS STILL THE 27TH December, and after my meditation Tom wished to go out.

This was a similar exercise to the Maiden Castle excursion, in that it was for us to improve our techniques for picking up vibration. We again were talking to each other, as well as to our Guides, so I will attempt to recount the event clearly, as the action moves between Astral Plane time and real time.

Tom had decided that he wanted to take me out for the day to Bradbury Rings, which was an old Roman fort situated at Kingston Lacey, between Wimbourne and Blandford in Dorset.

On arrival, it had the similar 'bubble feel' to that of Maiden Castle but not as strong. This fort is a lot smaller and is apparently where Arthur, my Gatekeeper, lived as a young soldier, with his family.

Today, Badbury Rings has trees growing on it, but in Arthur's day there were none, we were told.

When we arrived at the car park we could instantly tell that this was a lot smaller than the last fort, and lots of people were walking around with their families: children were playing with kites, elderly people were out for a stroll. People walking dogs were keeping to the outside fields, as dogs were forbidden to enter the main site. We walked through the kissing gate and up the path to the main entrance. We crossed an old Roman road, and as we did I could 'hear' the noise of soldiers, from years gone by, marching down the road in step, and I could see them in my mind's eye, dressed in their armour. The 'crunch, crunch' of their feet on the road as they marched in time together, was quite distinctive.

This time it was Arthur's turn to give us his tour. As we had done before, we walked anti-clockwise around the hillside, on the mound that was nearest the top of the hill, and in fact the outside edge of the rings.

It was another bitterly cold day with a cruel north wind that cut to the bone, fortunately we were all wrapped up in our warmest clothes. Other than the freezing elements, it was a pleasant winter's day.

Arthur explained that this had once been a busy fort. In its time it had witnessed hoards of people passing through, like a trading post, and you could wander around unnoticed, which was unlike Maiden Castle where it was more formal and almost needing an invite to visit.

The views were lovely and as we walked to the south, the wind dropped behind the trees and the air became warmer. The mounds were on a smaller scale but still a challenge to climb. Many people in many lifetimes had walked these mounds and half way round the south side, Arthur directed us into the trees and up a small path. We came to a halt at a spot on the right of the path.

"This is where my house was," Arthur announced.

Tuning in, I immediately felt warmer, as if standing inside his house, even though it wasn't there. I was being shown, in my mind's eye, inside a very modest little house. I could see Arthur's wife preparing a meal. A small table and chairs were positioned on one side, with a curtain pulled across to screen off the other side of the house, which I took to be sleeping accommodation.

Tom *in real time* rolled a cigarette. Arthur's youngest son asked what he was doing, and Tom just grinned and lit it up.

"He's smoking a cigarette," I tried to explain, but I don't think it was understood.

Arthur told us his house was south facing so that it caught the sun during the day as it was needed inside to bring warmth in the winter. I can believe that!

I thanked Arthur's wife for inviting us into her home and for making us feel welcome with her smiling warmth.

We moved off and sat on a bench outside, *in real time*.

Marie-Anne and William were very quiet on this trip. William hadn't visited the site before, and both he and Marie-Anne were interested in how Arthur used to live.

Tom's Gatekeeper was enjoying what he saw, and felt that it was a warmer climate than he had been used to as a Mongolian warrior.

We rejoined the path and carried on up the hill.

When we came to the gate to the east, we could feel the presence of the *past* inhabitants of this historic place, and felt we should step to one side so as not to obstruct the busy daily business.

Crowds were chatting, carts rumbling, children skipping along helping with the animals, all the hustle and bustle, sounds and smells, of a busy trading community.

Tom and I were amazed at what we were picking up. Margaret had taught us to listen and feel vibration. The whole bustling atmosphere was being conveyed to us both because we had learnt to 'tune in' and feel the ambiance.

Arthur then took us back up the mound and onto the outside edge of the hill. The wind cut though like a knife. He then directed us along a little further until we reached an ordnance survey stone, *in real time*, which points to possibly the old routes to Dorchester, Salisbury and Poole as the crow flies.

We turned down into the camp once again, behind the mound to the north. Here it felt a little warmer and we were more sheltered from the biting wind. Arthur led us up the main path. I'm sure my nose picked up on the scent of iron or metal being worked. Tom thought it may have been a working forge that had once been situated there, *in an earlier time.* Then we moved on to what I felt was a children's area, maybe a school for children to learn the traditions and ways of their time.

We moved on again. As we climbed the incline inside Badbury Rings, we approached another stone. This one had a circle on the top with a map engraved on it. We stopped to chat to another woman, *in real time,* who was enjoying the winter walk just as we were.

The sun was dropping even lower now and we felt it was time to go. Our trip out to Badbury Rings had been a pleasurable one. It had been a very different experience to the one at Maiden Castle. The hustle and bustle of a very busy community was what we had picked up on today.

We thanked Arthur, Spiritually, for showing us into his world and felt very honoured. It had been a lovely day and a very, very cold one too!

Tom decided to take some photographs of the setting sun, it was beautiful this evening and looked like a huge golden ball of fire.

Sorting Out the Fakes

14th January 2009

FOR THIS MEDITATION WE TRAVELLED back to Margaret's house. Margaret told us we were to go up onto the Astral Plane, cleanse ourselves in the waterfall and then go back to the tree of knowledge, where I would be shown 'four identical Marie-Anne's' and Tom would be shown 'four identical William's'. The task would be to pick out our true Guide from the vibration he/she would emit.

"Oh crikey!" I thought.

I glanced over to Tom who was looking a little worried.

Off we trotted in our usual fashion, up to the Astral Plane. There were hoards of people everywhere. The waterfall was cool and refreshing and I felt that maybe JC was in His usual place.

When I reached the tree I couldn't work out where my Marie-Anne's were, then realised I was to stand with my back to the tree. Sure enough, just as Margaret had said, I saw four Marie-Anne's, all standing in a row.

I approached the first one and to my surprise, instinct took over, and I started to scan her up and down and was able to absorb her energy, and then release it back out. That's the only way I can describe how I could 'feel' her and work out if she was my Guide or not.

Number One felt strange, so I moved onto number Two. The energy I felt from her was comfortable and familiar, like 'home' but just in case I was wrong, I moved on to number three to check her out. I did the same procedure, breathing her energy in and then releasing it out. It didn't feel as lovely as number two, so I decided she wasn't my Marie-Anne. Moving on to number four I sensed she was a very close match to number two.

I had a peek over at Tom. He looked as if he was chatting to his Guide, but we were told we were not to ask them anything as that would be cheating.

I scanned all four of my ladies again to see if I still came to the same conclusion: Marie-Anne was definitely number Two. Yes! And having made that decision, it felt ok to speak to her.

I asked if she could help me to see her more clearly, and for her to raise her volume as she was so quietly spoken. I know I can be a tad on the noisy side, and I sometimes miss things she is trying to tell me. It was weird. After I had asked her, my head felt like it was being put inside a goldfish bowl. My vision improved twofold. It felt like the lens on a microscope had been turned to focus better. She walked calmly around me, asking if it had improved. I could see her clearer than ever, especially her face with her mouth moving. I hoped this clearer picture of Marie-Anne would stay, but if it didn't, I knew now I just have to ask.

We were told that each of the Guides was holding a gift and when we had worked out which one was our true Guide, we were to accept the gifts they had to offer.

Marie- Anne gave me what looked initially, like a blue ball. Hmm!... now that's too easy, I thought. The second gift Marie- Anne gave me was a blue quarter moon. The third, a blue crown, made of wax or even a resin- type material. When it was placed on my head it seemed to just dissolve into me. What this meant I didn't know. Maybe I'm not supposed to have a crown, I'm not that good yet,

I thought! After that, I was given a deep blue coloured pyramid, which dissolved into my hand. I couldn't believe my luck because at Christmas I had gone in search for a pyramid crystal, just like that one, and I had wished for one, but unfortunately none of the crystal shops we had visited had stocked such a thing or had ever seen one.

The blue quarter moon now also seemed to have dissolved into my right hand.

I thanked the Marie-Anne's for the presents and for the enjoyable exercise. I knew number Two was my Guide, from her vibration.

It felt as if it was time to go back down into Margaret's living room. Once there, Margaret confirmed that my Guide was number Two.

"She felt like home," I explained to Margaret.

"Yes… And your gift?" Margaret asked

"It was blue," I said

"Yes," she replied. I could sense the excitement in her voice.

I told her what I had seen and Margaret was delighted. It was exactly what she had written down earlier that day, and stranger than that, when I drew the moon in the circle to show Margaret, it came out like a 3D orb. I felt that I should put a cross on the top. The gifts that were given were not actual gifts but symbolic gifts, of course.

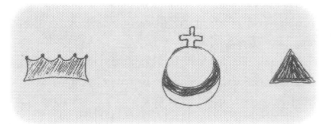

Later when we spoke to Sheryle about the orb, she laughed and explained that the cross and the orb were a joke amongst the Guides for Margaret, because apparently they call her the 'Upright Christian'.

YING AND YANG

OUR NEXT TASK TO DO that evening was a healing practice. Tom had only *received* healing, so this was a new experience for him to learn how to *give* healing energy to others. Also it was a new experience for me to work in this way.

Margaret wanted us to do healing with what she called 'Ying and Yang'. Also, as we were doing healing on Margaret, we were to look closely in front of us, because there would be three people. We were to concentrate and tell her, who these were.

Margaret explained to us that if two people work on one person, their energy is different, and it needs to be equalized. So to do this, Margaret told Tom and me to join our energy. She had us facing each other, holding our hands out in front, putting our right palm up and our left palm down. The energy flowed between our hands until it became equalised.

Margaret said, "This is known as Ying and Yang.

We had already asked for all our protection to be put into place, before the meditation that evening, so we didn't need to do it again and we could just start our healing.

Margaret was seated, and we needed to put her in alignment. To do this Tom placed his hands on her shoulders and asked his Gatekeeper to do the alignment. Energy flowed through Tom, and Margaret swayed around until she was aligned. Now we could begin our healing.

We scanned down over her body and stopped at her chest area. It felt dark and empty and in need of some lighter energy. This we brought in and the energy vibration changed to a lighter (in colour and feel) vibration. We carried on to the stomach, then realised we were not finished on the chest area, both our Guides told us to go back. We returned and remained there until we felt the area lighten and were told by our Guides to move on. It now felt softer.

We carried on down her body and under the seat of Margaret's chair. Later on Margaret told us it had felt like we were touching her bottom (our hands were well below her bottom I can tell you!) We carried on to her legs and feet, and finished with Tom putting Margaret in alignment again. As we worked our way from top to bottom, I had an inkling of who was standing in front of us.

I could see JC and Peter as clear as anything. In my mind's eye I could see that JC was standing in the middle with Peter, with his mop of dark hair, to the left. I remember him from when I first met Marie-Anne, and was wondering why this dark haired man was not coming closer to speak, only to find out later that this was not my Guide at all.

To JCs' right I could make out a man with a head of long, curly blonde hair. On asking his name I got 'Saul', but Margaret told me it was Simon, who brings peace.

On the morning of the meditation that Margaret had prepared for us, they had told her that we would see her late husband Bill, who was always around Margaret and who brought her great comfort. I have to be honest, I did not see him, but I do believe we will see him on our future visits to Margaret's home.

Apparently he was a lovely man who had made you feel very welcome. On arrival for the first time at Margaret's we had felt this. He had always offered tea to everyone who set foot in his home.

It was interesting what we had done this evening, with the energies as Ying and Yang, also trying to see what and/or who we could pick up on in the room. What Tom realized was that he also had the gift of being able to give!

I'm beginning to understand more as to why the Spirit world is getting us to do what we do. It is to become more aware of what is around us, and is fascinating.

ANGEL WINGS!

THIS PARTICULAR DAY, I WAS on my own and felt like just popping up to the Astral Plane to have a chat with Marie-Anne. I went up and met Marie-Anne by the tree. Beside her I saw something standing or quite possibly hovering, I wasn't too sure, and then I saw a huge Angel with magnificent wings. It wasn't a solid form that I could see before me, like Mary-Anne often appears (though there are occasions when she's not solid either, possibly when I'm not tuned in properly), but more of a smoke or ice, a translucent form. His lips were moving but I couldn't make out anything that was being said. I think I had seen him before, maybe he was the Angel I had spied sitting on the fence when Tom and I were off to the Indian village? They all look the same! I thought perhaps he was telling me his name was Gabriel, but it was all a bit unclear. I didn't think I was very tuned in to this Angel.

Then from out of no-where he gave me a set of beautiful wings which resembled the dainty little feathery wings that a hawk or some sort of small bird of prey have. Perhaps they were training wings or something? Bless! I thought they were brilliant and started to feel my feet lift off the path and down again. Wow! I liked this. I thought I'd have another go.

"Try," I heard the Angel say.

Honest to God, as true as I'm writing this, I felt myself rise again.

Here I was, fluttering off the ground with my learner wings and chatting to an Angel whom I thought was called Gabriel. I felt as if I wanted to give them a flap. They moved very silently and were compact and quick to respond. I felt ecstatic and very proud, and I felt myself lift higher and higher off the ground, above head height and gently back down again.

By thinking it, I could fly!

They felt so real, so a part of me. But I'm **no** Angel, I'm **only** human!

I thanked Marie-Anne and Gabriel and made my way back over to the mist and down through the trapdoor. I had a bit of trouble squashing my wings down with me but eventually ended up back in the familiar surroundings of my home. Funny though, I did feel like the wings were still there, and I did think it would be really interesting to know if Tom could see anything. It wouldn't surprise me, as he can see allsorts!

Since I was at home I could ask him straight away to have a close look at my colour and see if there was anything else. He looked, and said he could see purple on my cheeks and forehead, with splashes of silver and my gold aura, but that was it. I kept my Astral Plane excursion to myself and didn't tell him for days. I think they had just wanted me to have a go, and all in all it was a lovely experience and I felt very honoured, I realized the wings were only symbolic.!!

THE TUNNEL OF LIGHT

28th January 2009

I DROVE DOWN TO SEE MARGARET, solo. Tom had contracted a bug and didn't wish to pass it on, so he stayed tucked up at home. When I was sat in the cosy surroundings of Margaret's home, she started to tell me of this night's meditation.

"This one is a difficult one," she said seriously, "and what I want you to do is go up to the Astral Plane, go to the waterfall, meet your Guide by the tree, and for this meditation you must be completely silent. Do not make any sound whatsoever, for you will be shown a life. Observe everything, but to start Marie-Anne will give you the cloak of invisibility. Put it around yourself and then she will take you into the tunnel of light, where you will be shown the life. When finished, Marie-Anne will touch your arm and that will be your signal to leave. You will be taken back to the tree and when you have reached it, you will need to take off your cloak and give it back to Marie-Anne. Only then will you be able to ask questions or talk to Marie-Anne."

I was really excited and definitely up for the challenge. The green mist seemed to form quickly as up I went. It did feel strange without

Tom by my side. I followed Margaret's instructions and met Marie-Anne by the tree, cloak in hand. It's always so lovely to see her, and as always a warm day here, a pleasant change from the cold spell we've been having in real time.

Marie-Anne passed me the cloak. It was pure white and similar to the Scottish Widow style cloak she has herself. I like these you know!

I pulled the hood over my head so I was completely covered. Lowering my head I couldn't see very well at all, I had no idea where she was leading me. Marie-Anne held my hand and Guided me to the tunnel of light. Sure enough, I could soon see light all around me and I felt I was being taken down a long tunnel. It felt safe and warm and glorious.

Colours were passing me, like orbs of light travelling to their destination.

As I'm writing this I'm being made aware of the place where I was in the meditation. I believe I had been taken to the tunnel of light that is visible on a person's passing from this world to the next, and the coloured orbs were the souls on their way to heaven.

This is such a massive realization I just can't find the words to express how it felt. I continue to be in awe of it all. I realised this was why I was not to make any sound and to remain invisible.

Margaret had told me that when you speak, the vocal chords vibrate and it's **this** vibration that other souls will pick up. So by 'talking' (in my head) I may be responsible for disrupting their pathway.

Marie-Anne came to a stop and I tried to focus, but I couldn't see very well. I tried as hard as I could to pick up on something, then it became slightly clearer. I could see arms and legs of a child or a young man, then I thought I saw a girl and a boy, and could pick out the back of a young child. I could make out a young man on a horse saying goodbye to his loved one.

The next picture was that of a big man dressed in armour and a helmet that came down over the nose. He was in a huge, flat field with a castle on the top of the hillside behind him. I felt it was in England, Scotland or France.

Then I saw a room with the soldier lying in a bed. He was still fully dressed in armour and I wondered if it was his deathbed. Was this my Arthur? He didn't look Roman. The man was lying motionless.

I felt Marie-Anne touch my arm so this was my signal to leave. I was a bit confused, and couldn't see a great deal.

We floated back through the tunnel of light and back up to the tree. I had felt I should take shallow breaths to be as quiet as possible, during this meditation, now I could take a deep breath and bring back my normal breathing. I removed the cloak, folded it up and handed it back to Marie-Anne.

"Was it Arthur I saw?" I asked.

"Yes," came the reply, at least I think that's what I heard.

I couldn't wait to tell Margaret, and made my way back to the trapdoor after thanking Marie-Anne for her help. I took myself back into Margaret's sitting room and opened my eyes, only to find that Margaret was still in meditation.

Oh no! She's not ready yet, I thought. She's still up there! I thought I had better go back quickly.

This I did, and found Marie-Anne still by the tree, now with my beautiful Bear, my power animal. I thought I had asked all I could and couldn't think of anything else to say.

"Make your way to the green mist," I heard Margaret say quietly, so I said another goodbye to Marie-Anne and departed.

"What did you see?" Margaret enquired.

I was so excited and related all the details.

She frowned, looked confused and instructed me to return to the Astral Plane, and take a closer look at what I had first seen.

I was able to close my eyes and immediately return to my meditation. I scrutinised the scene and could see a girl and a boy. Well, they all look the same from behind when they're young don't they, boys and girls?

Margaret spoke out loud, "Right, concentrate on the girl. What do you see?"

I saw a blue dress and shoes, and a hair-band with a butterfly on it.

"It's a bow," Margaret explained. "Now look around her. What do you see?"

I looked intently. I could see about six to eight people all wearing dark clothes. The ceiling was very low in the room and it was all very dark and dreary.

"What expressions do they have on their faces?" asked Margaret.

I could see a little girl's bed…. her deathbed. The people, her family I presumed, looked defeated, and I felt a sense of hopelessness. They were stood at the foot and side of her bed, all very quiet and forlorn. There was no crying or movement from any of the relatives, only a sense of loss.

Then, the most wondrous and truly beautiful sight occurred. A beam of light appeared and I saw her soul or her essence, call it what you like, leave her body like a fine wisp of smoke, rising gently out of her body. It was so, inexplicably beautiful, like a thousand tiny diamonds glistening in the light as it softly rose from the entire length of her body all at the same time.

It wasn't a human form that left, just wispy strands that made me think of a butterfly being set free from its casing.

"Well done!" Margaret exclaimed. "You have been shown the life of a child in the 1930s. Her family were very poor and she died of starvation. That's why there was the sense of helplessness among her family members.

Tragedy!

I was left feeling that there must be a better life or a better place for the little girl's soul to go to now.

I had felt a bit of a failure for not getting it right at first, and felt I had fluffed it up by not listening properly.

"Not at all," Margaret reassured me. "You got there the second time, so well done."

She continued, "Now I have something else for you to do. Fill the room with pink light and make a huge pink bubble. Inside it will be someone. Tell me who it is. They will have a message for me. Listen to the message and then tell me."

"Not much then," I laughed, but was keen to have a go.

To my surprise, the bubble appeared quickly and I could see a form. It was one I had seen before. He was blonde, young looking, with wavy shoulder length hair and wonderful strong looking shoulders!

"It's ...Sss...Sss..Sss..Sss" I spluttered, not quite able to get the word out

"Yes!" Margaret encourage, "Sss is right..."

"Sssssssssssssssssssssssssssssssssimon!" I spat out!!

"Yes, it's Simon," Margaret confirmed. "Now what's he wearing?"

I had no idea, as I couldn't see very well, so I asked Margaret to help me.

"Well tell him to come closer," Margaret laughed.

He did, and I could see a simple v–necked woven tunic. It was plain but tied with a rope around his waist and stopped just above his knees.

"Yes, now ask him for his message."

"Tell her to get the kettle on," came the reply as quick as a flash. I repeated this to Margaret.

"Tell him not to be facetious!" Margaret laughed.

I listened for more but could not hear, however I could see a picture in my mind's eye. I could see Margaret and Sheryle sitting at the kitchen table in Margaret's house.

"Yes, what are we talking about?"

Shopping, came into my head like a flash. I passed this on to Margaret.

"Yes! Where?"

"Newquay," was the reply I thought I heard.

"Close," she said. "A little more…"

"Newton Abbott," I blurted out, letting logic get in the way.

"No!" she retorted.

"New…New…New," I was trying too hard now, and was still very excited about my success after the failure of the first meditation.

"Don't worry," Margaret consoled. "Go on, try again."

I asked Marie-Anne to help.

I then saw green woven fabric in a fabric shop. It was as if I was looking through a doorway into a material shop and seeing rolls and rolls of different coloured fabric on shelves. The green fabric was being placed on a counter in front of me. It was only a piece, of the fabric, that was important for some reason. .

"Don't know what that is," Margaret said.

I replied, "It's part of the fabric."

"Don't worry, carry on," Margaret urged.

I could make out an object that was a blue ceramic kind of object. I felt that if I flicked it with my fingers it would 'ting'. Margaret again wasn't sure what I was picking up on and suggested it could be a vase of some sort.

"This much I will tell you," Margaret started. "This afternoon, Sheryle and I were sitting in my kitchen at the table. Sheryle and her husband own a paint company and they have invented a paint that glows in the dark. A chemical company is testing it up to EU standards. They are hoping that British Rail will be interested in it. If they make money from their invention, we are all going shopping to…. New York!

Whoopee!!

I was on another high here and now, so joyous that I had done so well tonight and for getting the first part of their destination. Margaret was pleased with me too, and suggested that we put the kettle on for that cuppa.

As we were enjoying our brew, I glanced at Margaret's notice board where there was a leaflet with a green colour to it, which was the same colour as the fabric I had seen. Almost a granny smith colour, I explained.

Margaret wracked her brains but still couldn't throw light on any of it. We continued our chat about our evening's events then said our goodbyes as I headed home.

The next morning I woke up with the answer. Part of the fabric of America is the Big Apple...New York!

I couldn't wait to get on the phone to Margaret to tell her.

"Grace, well done!" she laughed with delight.

I was so proud of myself, and spent the rest of the day with a huge smile on my face!

Which Pathway?

February 11th 2009

THIS EVENING, WARM IN THE comfort of Margaret's home, we were met with her announcement, "Tonight will be a hard one, but I think you can manage it. What I would like you to do is go up and meet your Guides who will take you over the bridge, not to the Indian village but to a series of pathways. Now what you have to do is: when you reach each fork in the road, feel the vibration and choose which path to take. You must *not* ask your Guides."

And so off we went. We walked over to the waterfall and then to the tree. I saw Margaret with a group talking to JC and as I passed them I noticed a gentleman with short blonde hair whom I hadn't seen before. Marie-Anne was waiting for me and we walked over to the bridge. I could see clumps of pretty flowers growing around the bridge and over on the other side.

When we reached the other side of the bridge I couldn't see anything whatsoever to start with as it was completely dark. I thought if I kept walking I would eventually come to a path or bump into something. All of a sudden I saw a grassy bank with ferns and some primroses growing on it. The way forward seemed to open up into two paths going left and right. Around the path wasn't clear and all I could see was a murky darkness.

Standing on the left pathway with Margaret's words in my head, I let the vibration of the pathway wash over me like a draught. It felt cold and dark.

I stood in front of the right- hand one and it felt warm and light, so I went to the right. For a fleeting second I caught sight of an Angel, then a blue-white lantern that seemed to light the way. I carried on walking down the path for what seemed like ages, and saw some flowers in small clumps resembling Busy Lizzies, growing by the side of the path.

I reached another fork on my journey, this time the left one felt fuzzy, so I turned right again, feeling it as the 'softest' and seemed to have a waterfall off to the right. I was a little apprehensive: this was not easy, going just with what you felt. Logic kept creeping in and sometimes I wasn't sure if it's what I was feeling or merely what I thought I should be feeling. I had to throw logic out and that's hard.

I kept on walking and reached yet another fork. This time I would go left I decided, after all, I hadn't gone left yet, it seemed ok and I thought I'd give it a go! It felt like I was walking downwards into a tunnel or a cave a little way, then the vibration quickly felt cold. It made me feel very uncomfortable and I didn't like it, so I back –tracked up the tunnel to the fork, and set off on the right hand path to try again.

I could see the path was now leading me to a garden with steps up into it, not stone steps but earth ones. These led me through what appeared to be a gate, with a hedge either side of a garden. I carried on walking down the path, which led me to such a delightful, peaceful place. In the distance, a beautiful lake could be seen, with a path leading in that direction, but before it there was yet another fork and another path to choose.

I thought that what I could already see was a stunning view and it looked safe, so with this in mind, I took the left path because it was visible, and dismissed the right- hand one, as I couldn't see it properly.

I walked on down the sunny path, past beautiful Scot's pines making attractive shade as on a summer's day. I thought I felt the presence of my Bear for some reason, although I didn't see him.

By this time, the path had made its way along the side of the lake, and I was thoroughly enjoying the stunning view which reminded me of a Scottish lock, but then....it changed.... all of a sudden! I felt it had all turned prickly, horribly prickly, so that was my cue to back- track, and fast. I retraced my steps as quickly as I could, back up the path to the fork at the top, and then headed off down the right hand path.

This side felt calm, warm and welcoming, thank goodness, and in fact was a continuation of the garden with trimmed hedges and magical pathways enticing me to explore more. As I walked further along, I could see the most attractive light. It was situated in what seemed to be a circular courtyard at the entrance to a special building of some kind. I had a sense of not really being permitted to proceed any further. I did feel that I had now reached the correct destination.

"Make your way to the green mist, through the green door," spoke a familiar voice.

Green door? What green door? I thought, and then before my eyes, there was a green door. I didn't think I would make it back through the different paths, so was very grateful to have a short cut.

The door opened easily and I was back at the hatch, just like magic.

I thanked Marie-Anne for her guidance and because I hadn't had chance to ask questions this time, I wasn't sure if what I had seen and felt was correct. I said goodbye and stepped into the familiar green mist and down into my body and Margaret's lounge.

"Well Tom, how did you get on?" Margaret asked

"It was a disaster. I didn't see a thing and it was all foggy." He looked a bit disappointed and my heart went out to him.

"Grace?" she asked

I relayed what I had seen which delighted Margaret. I was happy because I had thought I hadn't seen things too clearly. She was pleased that I had gone with what eventually 'felt' right, and had seen the blue and white light which was Margaret's staff apparently. The Angel could have possibly been Margaret before she had put her cloak of invisibility on, and of course, sensing the presence of my Bear who keeps popping up for no apparent reason.

The white light was from the Roman villa where, apparently, Tom's mum now lives since she passed over.

As for Tom, he was to go back and have another go, just like I had done the week before. On his second attempt he collected all the information William had prepared for him.

Another valuable lesson in 'vibration' had been learnt. The last path had looked idyllic I had gone with what I had *seen*. I hadn't taken notice of the vibration that was being given to me. I chose to walk the path that **looked** good, and not the one with the vibration that *felt* good.

The lesson: all is not always, as it seems.

In life, you must go with what is *felt,* because vibration is the truth. Pay less attention to what the eyes tell you, sometimes they only see the glamour and glitz and you can easily be fooled.

A Plan for the Future

22nd Febuary 2009

I WAS FEELING A LITTLE 'LOST' and in need of some positive input, and felt a trip to the Astral Plane would help, but not before a good cleansing. During the week I had picked up a cold and had to cancel my clients' appointments.

I asked Arthur to put me in alignment and felt myself being swayed around. It felt as if I was well out. I also thought it might be a good idea to do some ball cleansing.

The balls that came through were orange and turquoise, and then I felt a strange vibration as a purple one came down which turned into seven balls, all turning anti-clockwise and then clockwise. These balls then appeared to change into one beam of purple light. It was quite a colourful show.

After this it was up in the green mist and over to the waterfall. No sooner had I started to cleanse myself in the water when JC started speaking to me about a plan to help others.

In my minds eye, JC was presenting me with some pictures of premises that had lots of rooms, apparently for healing and tuition, similar to a retreat venue. Next He showed me many faces of genuinely good-hearted people I know. He was telling me more and more, so much I couldn't take it all in. I felt as if I needed to draw up a plan on paper and JC was instructing me to go back down and write it up, so I descended through the trapdoor and searched for a pen and paper and then waited quietly. This is what came through:

Honest healing and teaching; premises in an old building; to be properly managed with people working from the heart not just wanting a wage packet at the end of the week; people wishing to help others and make a difference, they in turn would be paid a wage, so they would not be taken advantage of; fees, of course, will need to be charged for the treatments; the remaining proceeds after running costs was to go to humanitarian projects helping others.

I thanked J.C for his ideas.

I have noticed the people that have been shown to me from JC are people who have a very special feel about them. Maybe these people hold the keys for certain aspects of this plan, I don't know yet.

It is all very exciting. I just have to feel for the right paths to get started.

"You're already on it," is the message coming through as I write this. I feel its Arthur my Gatekeeper talking to me.

"Keep focused, girl, it *is* possible!"

Wow! I hope so. I don't mind admitting, exciting as it feels, it is still a big step to take and almost exciting to the extent that it is frightening!

I'm pleased to think that some of the managerial and organisational skills that I have gleaned along the way might actually now come in handy.

"They sure will!" I hear.

I am compelled to say thank-you over and over again.

"You're welcome, it's a pleasure" is the voice I hear.

Goodness...... I hope this all will one day come true.

Over the following weeks I found myself picking up little ideas here and there, and writing them down, so that I can refer to them at a later date. I've jotted down bits of information about the people I've come across since my journey with Margaret. I'm just taking note of who they are, what they do, and how they feel, because I think that later on these people could be the important 'keys'. You just never know!

BILL

25th February 2009

WHENEVER WE ARRIVE AT MARGARET'S she is very welcoming, and the first thing she does is makes us both a lovely cup of tea. Tom and Margaret always have a cigarette and we all have a chat. This week we talked about the plan that I had been shown and which I had discussed with Margaret on another occasion, by phone. Now, having brought it with me, Margaret could see it on paper.

Sheryle had had messages come through which had confirmed what I had seen. As we were talking, I could feel this warmth on my back, as if someone had placed an arm around me.

"Who's there?" I asked Margaret

"It's Bill," grinned Margaret. Bill was her husband who had passed away.

"What is he telling you?" she asked me.

I tried hard to listen but couldn't hear him, so asked Marie-Anne to help.

"I see broccoli," I said, uncertainly.

"Yes, he loved it," she replied, "I hated it."

"I see lots of vegetables and stew and dumplings," I reported.

"Well done, I've made some this afternoon," she said, pointing to a large saucepan on her range.

"I see brown shoes!" I exclaimed, now I was on a roll. "They seem like ladies shoes with a heel."

"Look closer at the heel," she suggested.

They seemed to change into a man's brogue. I could see it clearer now and the shoe was very shiny, as if it had been highly polished. It looked almost like ox blood in colour.

"Yes!" Margaret said. She went on to explain that Bill had once owned a very expensive pair of shoes. (They were Scottish) and an old friend who appreciated good quality shoes had told her husband they would outlive him, and that he could wear them in his coffin. When he became ill, not to be outdone by a pair of brogues, he threw them away, just to outlive them! We all laughed. How funny is that!

Next, I picked up on one trouser leg. It was a dark charcoal colour and neatly pressed.

"Yes, that was the suit he wore. He wasn't particularly fond of it. It also had a pinstripe design".

I didn't pick out the finer details, only the colour but then suddenly caught sight of a cream bag with two pearls on the front made of some sort of satin fabric.

"Ha, now he's having a laugh!" Margaret chuckled. "He used to complain that his pockets were always bulging with bits and bobs of mine. I hate handbags! He used to complain that I was ruining the lining of his suits with all of my stuff and he wanted me to get myself a handbag to match a pearl necklace I had, but I wouldn't hear of it."

I was gob smacked. Oh my goodness! Had I really picked up all of this? I was amazed.

Then I saw an old fashioned globe, the ones that have the brown parched paper and fancy writing. I saw it on a table, and a hand pointing to the Northern Hemisphere. I wasn't able to pick out the specific country as it was spinning.

"This may be related to the change in the earth that is currently being discussed," Margaret told us.

My next picture was that of two comfy chairs, positioned next to a lovely open fire that was burning logs. I could smell the smoke from it, and it looked comforting and welcoming. There was a table next to the chairs. I was seeing an evening scene with the fire lit.

"That's our old house," Margaret explained. "He's showing you the sitting room. Well done Grace, you've done really well," she praised.

"It just happened and I can't believe it! There was one picture after another!" I was completely overwhelmed by it all. "There's more of it coming too! I now see forget-me- nots, snowdrops, primroses and daffodils!" I explained excitedly.

"Well, I'm not likely to be forgetting him now am I?"

She smiled, "He's showing you the garden. It was full of flowers."

"Red Camellia," I declared.

"I can't believe you have just said that!" Margaret looked surprised and went on to explain that when they had moved into the house, there was a huge red Camellia growing on the patio. It was so big that they eventually trimmed it into a tree.

Now it was my turn to be surprised. It had all just come like a bolt out of the blue!

Have Another Go!

That same evening Margaret had more for us to do. Before we embarked on another meditation, Margaret had a 'helpful hint' for us, as she called it.

The hint was not to let logic kick in when you are meditating.

Apparently, by pressing the right hand nostril, it will slow down the left hand side of the brain, the logic side, and allow the right hand side of the brain to dominate. This is the side we don't use so often and is the side used to communicate with Spirit.

Well I'll give anything a go, so thanked Margaret for the hint.

We settled down for our meditation.

"Tonight is another challenging one," Margaret announced. "I would like you to go up onto the Astral Plane, meet your Guides, and Tom, with your back against the tree of knowledge, you will need to go left and you, Grace, need to go off to the right with Marie-Anne. There will be someone special for each of you to see in your own meditation. Look around and observe as much as possible. There will be something relative to you, at this moment, in your life."

With these instructions on board I couldn't wait to get started, so up onto the Astral Plane Tom and I went.

Marie-Anne was there waiting, and after cleansing myself we walked off to the right together. There appeared to be a path to the right of the waterfall. As we walked along, a dense wood stood majestically to our left. I could feel grass at first, under my feet, and a metal bar across my arm. Looking down I saw what seemed to be a metal handle across my right arm, with a bucket or a cauldron attached to it. Its colour was black and it was getting heavier and heavier. Inside, I thought I could see gold or a gold light coming from the depths, but wasn't sure. It was so heavy, I couldn't carry on, and was almost tripping over it as it bumped and banged against my legs.

Suddenly I was surrounded by dozens of children, and it felt like they were pulling me forwards by my hands, along with the bucket.

The next thing I knew we were at the beach. It had a tropical feel with white sand and palm trees, and also what looked to be a vegetation area, with trees behind it. To my left, there were really fancy sunshades, all very posh looking, and over to my right some red ordinary ones as well. The sea appeared to be a light turquoise colour and crystal clear. It was gorgeous.

Behind us was my big Bear, bumbling along as usual, showing no concern for his surroundings and strolling along looking very comfortable and 'hip' in his…

Oh no, surely not…

Sunglasses?…..

And was that a smile I could see on his face?

The children were happily playing and running around on the sand. The sound of their giggles and laughter was a treasure from heaven. It's not until your children have grown up and left home you truly realize what a beautiful sound it is.

In front of me was a small pontoon with a boat.

It looked as if we were in the midst of sharing a picnic with the children one minute, then in my arms I had suddenly become aware of the fact that I was carrying bundles of sandwiches wrapped in patterned tablecloths.

We sat down and I felt we were now on a boat. I secretly hoped it wasn't going to be a long journey as I'm prone to the odd bout of sea sickness. I definitely don't have sea–legs, that's for sure.

The children were full of excitement. Peering into the crystal clear water I could see a dolphin and a manatee swimming in the depths. The sunlight glistened and bounced like silver splashes on top of the water.

"Five minutes," said Margaret.

Blimey, I thought, now that's all gone rather quickly, I had really been enjoying myself.

Back on shore, I bid farewell to the children and Marie-Anne. I didn't want to leave one bit. I could sense the children not really wanting me to go either, and had a feeling I was taking these children on holiday.

Anyway, my time was up, so I reluctantly made my way back to the green mist that was waiting for me and descended to join Margaret and Tom.

Tom was to retell his story first:

He had seen his mum and an old school mate who had died in a motorcycle accident not long after leaving school. His mum was admiring Tom's blue motorbike that had appeared all clean and shiny, and he had had an enjoyable time. His mum had asked if he might take her for a ride sometime when it was warmer, bless her.

Margaret then turned to me and I related what I had seen.

"No," she said. "That is Not it". There are children up there, lots of children and they are all very excited because you are visitors on the Astral Plane. They have seen your bright light, which is similar to Sheryle's and mine, and they have grabbed you quickly and pulled you along. Now off you go back up and try again."

Oh dear, I thought. I'd really messed up big time! So tail between my legs, I took myself back up on the Astral Plane and had another go. This time I could see flowers, and my dad who was dressed in a white robe with gold laurel leaves, resembling a Greek band, in his hair. He was wearing sandals and was standing next to a unicorn, which looked so white and soft. I felt as if I could reach out and touch it with my fingertips, and I could even see the hairs moving. Now that was weird.

Dad walked towards me with his all-so-familiar-limp. I thought that everything was supposed to be 'fixed' when we passed over to the other side, and that your ailments and pain were no more. Then he started running backwards and forwards on the lawn.

"Look, they've fixed it!" he laughed. I must admit, he looked like he ran with no effort at all.

Both dad and the unicorn were next to a building that looked as if it had a glow about it. I felt like I needed to say goodbye to dad, it was a very quick visit. I did so and set off to the green mist, and back again into Margaret's living room for the second time that evening.

I took a deep breath and relayed my experience.

Apparently it was Tom's unicorn I had caught sight of, Margaret explained, and told me that I shouldn't have seen it. I should have seen a building and should have entered it. I looked up at Margaret's face and was met with an expression that I had witnessed before, and thought oh gawd! I've gone and done it wrong again....

"Go back again and go in the building," she told me.

Back up on the Astral Plane for the third time that evening, tail well and truly lodged between my legs, head hung low and feeling as if I was doing a walk of shame.

"You are the weakest link good bye!" came to mind.

Margaret and Tom had long ago vacated the room, off to the kitchen for a well earned cup of tea and a cigarette.

I prayed madly for help in any shape or form. This time I saw light coloured double doors with patterns engraved on them. They opened. Inside was a huge hall with a black and grey marble floor that had been highly polished. Leading off from my right and left were two more corridors, both long and straight and looked never- ending.

I felt I needed to go straight on and there was a bright light surrounding me.

Then I could see two stone lions, or were they gold? When I approached them, they seemed to be moving, which made me jump.

In front was a minstrel's gallery staircase. A door to my left was shut tightly and I knew that was out of bounds.

Beyond the right hand side staircase was a corridor, where on the left the first door was open. Inside was a dining room with a big window that let in the light, and a magnificent table which had thirteen chairs around it.

I moved on along the corridor and went down a couple of steps, entering what appeared to be a vast hall with pillars in the centre. It had a huge ceiling decorated with elaborate gold patterns. Several sets of tall French doors stretched along the whole of one side, letting more light in, flooding the wooden floor. It all gave the impression of being very grand. At the far end was a massive fireplace, which was not lit.

To the right of that fireplace there appeared to be more of the corridor. The next door on the left was open and what appeared to be a dormitory or hospital- type ward inside. It looked very clean and white, almost sterile, with the old iron framed hospital beds. White blankets were neatly made up on the beds with perfect square 'hospital corners'. I couldn't get over how pristine it all looked.

Beyond this, along the corridor I could make out another room, and I felt I was being shown a kitchen with herbs in it, for medicine or food, waiting to be processed. On the side was a pestle and mortar and chopped herbs in jars and bottles. It was all quite fascinating.

By now, I felt exhausted and needed to get to the green mist. My brain felt totally drained, the batteries were running low. I hoped and prayed that this time I had managed to get it right.

"Oh well done!!" Margaret exclaimed when I told her what I had seen.

Thank God for that, I thought! Margaret explained that I was being shown a pathway which was to come, sometime in the future.

"That cauldron containing the gold light which you found so heavy is your 'pot of gold': the house and what you provide for others.

She went on to tell us, "You and Tom will purchase a country house. I think it is somewhere in a poor country. I think it is an orphanage. The room with beds is a dormitory and the kitchen is one that will be used for healing remedies. Sheryle has also had messages telling her of a place of excellence that is to be opened up in the Chamberly, or Salwayminster area, that will be based on your teachings."

Both Tom and I looked at each other.

Oh my goodness! I thought, looks like we will be passing on our skills then.

Sheryle had apparently also said, "When a Native American enters the White House, the world will start to change. There will be a re-distribution of wealth. The greedy will lose the wealth, and those who are willing to help others will have it given to them."

Quite an amazing sequence of events to come! Time will tell....

Both Tom and I left Margaret's that evening with warmth in our hearts for our special teacher, and Spirit Guides.

WHICH FLIGHT?

28th February 2009

TOM HAS A NUMBER OF gifts, one of which is to have a very clear line of communication with his Guide William. On this particular evening in our own home, it was Tom's turn to lead a meditation for me. It made a nice change for us, and an opportunity for him to get on with his homework.

He said it would also help me to see colours more easily. I was happy with this, as it's not something I find as easy as Tom does, and I could definitely do with a bit of practice.

"You are to go up and see Marie-Anne on the Astral Plane, she will take you to visit a famous aircraft," he explained. "You are to make note of its name, colour and its number. You need to observe your surroundings, and see if you can find something of mine that looks 'out of place'. When you have done all of this, come back down and tell me what you have seen."

I was raring to go and very excited as usual, so off I went with a hop and a skip and saw Marie-Anne waiting by the tree. I went to the waterfall then back to her, and noticed William, and Tom's

Gatekeeper, on the opposite side of the path. We all marched over the bridge.

At first I didn't really notice anything, but I did have a 'feeling' that I was next to a World War Two aeroplane. Gradually I picked out a grey fuselage, a rounded nose, and a cockpit on the top with glass for the roof. Then I picked out four propellers and a woman painted on the side under the window. The word "Belle" kept on jumping out at me. Underneath the plane I could see what looked like bomb doors, open, and showing me where the bombs would have been dropped from. The back of the plane wasn't very clear to me. Right from the start, when I was first looking the plane over, I had sensed an almost 'prickly vibration', and now it was growing stronger.

Was that my Bear sat in the cockpit? Oh my! He was wearing goggles and looking, by all sense and purpose, like he was preparing himself for take-off! Well, if he's flying, I'm off. I don't want to be in the plane with him at the controls, that's for sure! I felt a sudden sense of urgency to vacate the area. I needed to make my way back down through the trapdoor, and on my way I kept trying to think of the numbers. All I got in my mind was the number 1943.

I told of my findings to Tom.

"No, that wasn't it," he said. Tom then went on to explain that **be** had in fact been listening to a radio program that morning, which had been discussing those sorts of aircraft. It was called 'The Memphis Belle', but that wasn't what I was supposed to find at all.

Those all too familiar words echoed in my ears: "Go back and have another go." This time it was from Tom, not Margaret!

Off I went again; the word 'determination' didn't even come close.

This time I saw an aircraft with a pointed nose. Well, it had to be Concorde. It was painted red white and blue on the tail, with the main body painted white. I walked around it and on the opposite side saw a huge green ribbon along its length. I got the words British Airways, and 'Gladys'. I wasn't sure where the Gladys fitted in to it at all; maybe it was a nickname from the flight crew who looked after her or something. Inside I saw rows of seats, and Marie-Anne and I walked up the aisle towards the cockpit. The cabin contained dials and instruments of all kinds, covering all surfaces. I was surprised it was quite small and cramped.

Looking forward, I could see the nose bent downwards, enabling me to see out of the aircraft window. It was parked up with grass around it, like it was out to pasture.

We turned around and walked back down the aisle, passing what I can only describe as something that looked like 'dossers corner!' Tom's Gatekeeper was stretched out in one of the chairs, his huge feet straight out in front, and his hands resting on the animal skins on his big stomach, snoozing! Tom's power animal, his wolf, had made himself at home, curled up in one of the seats opposite his Gatekeeper, facing them and the back of the plane, was my Bear, slouched in a seat with his huge hairy paws behind his head and his feet outstretched. Looking closer, I could see something white lying across his stomach, but didn't see exactly what.

On another seat, I was drawn to what looked like a blue pyramid, similar to a gift I had received a while ago, and then a white light, or an orb, beside it, which I felt I was not to touch. I tried my last task which was to pick up on any number, but couldn't find one. Then it suddenly felt it was time to go.

It had all gone by so quickly. I thanked Marie-Anne, and I made my way back to the green mist and back down to our sitting room.

"Concorde," I said to Tom in triumph.

"Yes," he replied.

"Gladys?" I queried

"That may be what the pilots called it, but I have no idea," answered Tom.

"British Airways, red, white and blue?"

"Yes," Tom smiled.

Thank goodness for that I thought, and went on to tell him about the 'gathering in dosser's corner.'

Tom was observing me up on the Astral Plane, to see if I was doing as he had instructed, so he was well aware of what had gone on. He explained that when Marie-Anne and I were walking towards the cockpit, my Bear was walking behind us pushing a trolley, wiggling his bum with his aviator goggles still on, and wearing an apron and a little hat. Tom said he looked like a 'trolley dolly!!' We creased up laughing.

It was funny, because as Tom had finished saying this, I could see in my mind's eye Tom's wolf peering out of one eye, studying my Bear as he plonked himself down on the seat near him. He was just keeping note of all events going on, my Bear still had his uniform on.

The 'out of place' item Tom had asked me to find, I thought, was an orb. Tom said that when I was given my blue pyramid on a previous meditation, he had been given a gold ball. That was what I was to find. We concluded that 'help' had been offered in the way that both items were put together for a 'prompt'. The number, I really didn't have a clue about, and apparently this Concorde was given the number 002, and there is one based in France with the number 001.

Tom did go on to tell me I had, in fact, walked through this aircraft on a visit to Yeovilton air museum once. On that particular occasion, we had looked at so many and it was years ago, when the children were small; my memories were all a bit vague and I didn't remember.

Tom was delighted that I eventually got the meditation correct, and the green ribbon had been placed around the plane when it was first launched, apparently. I felt quite chuffed with myself.

A Bit of a telling Off

I SPOKE WITH MARGARET YESTERDAY AND had a bit of a telling off, to say the least. Apparently, I have been racing on ahead, and leaving my poor Guide Marie-Anne behind, not waiting for her or listening to what she has to tell me, which is what I should be doing.

I was mortified. That poor lady, what have I done to her?! This is why I have had to go back to the Astral Plane several times. Apparently they knew what I would be like up there, explained Margaret, so they put Marie-Anne with me to quieten me down. Poor soul has got one massive task on her hands -- when I get excited about something, I think I must resemble a ping pong ball on a piece of elastic!

I was just so eager to learn.

All I wanted to do was get it done and to do the right thing. Now I had gone and insulted the one person who was given to me to help, and she had now taken a step back, apparently.

This was why I was having trouble hearing her. I was babbling on and making so much noise, the poor girl couldn't be heard!

I felt the only honourable thing to do was to go up onto the Astral Plane and apologise, and the sooner the better, Margaret also explained that she herself hadn't known how to put it to me, without bursting my bubble, bless her. I'm happy I have now been told, because without Marie-Anne's guidance I would miss important details.

When we next arrived at Margaret's home I was very remorseful, and told her I'd come with my tail between my legs. Margaret came towards me her arms outstretched, and gave me a big hug.

"The last thing I wanted to do was to hurt you, "she said.

I felt a bit better then, and she gave me a big smile. "I have a lovely meditation for you this evening, Grace," she said, still smiling.

Tom was to do a different one. Margaret went on to explain that Spirit wanted to see how far I would go without listening to Marie-Anne.

Apparently I had now gone far enough on my own.

Margaret explained that in the last meditation Marie-Anne had been on my left, and behind me, when we went off to the lovely building that is apparently the dream lodge.

Any Guide will retreat if you are not listening to them, so if they are on your left, there is something wrong; something that you are doing or not doing.

On reflection, during the meditation (of the planes) that Tom did for me, Marie- Anne was telling me something was wrong: that was the prickly vibration I was sensing.

"Live and learn, girl," has just come in from someone as I am writing this!

"Grace, you are to go up and to go to the waterfall. Meet Marie-Anne under the tree. Sit there and she will come to you. You are to stay there with her and not say anything at all. Just sit with her and feel her vibration and listen to her. Look around and say nothing. Take a note of everything you see and hear." Margaret directed.

I took myself up to the Astral Plane…. slowly, double checking everything I possibly could, and made my way to the waterfall. Walking along the path, I could still hear the scrunching of the stones beneath my feet and see the brown path, standing out in contrast to the green of the grass. It felt lovely and warm; it was like a summer's day.

I made my way across the embankment to the stones, and up to the waterfall. As I stood under the water, I could feel it wash over my front, and I could see the light sparkle through it, and for the first time, it felt cold. I turned and did my back, still feeling the cold. I then slowly and carefully stepped out and I made my way back over the stones and back to the tree, still feeling a bit chilled as I sat down to wait for Marie-Anne.

I noticed a brown mouse, just as I had when I had first gone up to the Astral Plane. That first time I had felt a presence, and now I had felt it again, and she was indeed behind me. I felt Marie-Anne's hands on my shoulders. I sat with my head bowed, my eyes closed, and I listened.

I felt a vibration go right down over my body; it was quite strong and this only re-enforced the feeling that I was still quite cold. After a minute or two it changed to a beautiful warm glow, which made me feel as if I was in a warm bath, or even a bubble bath. This feeling stayed with me for some time, and I felt Marie-Anne beside me and back in her rightful position on my right. I could see her grey skirt with the white apron of her top tunic. She appeared young to me at first, and then older, and I did get the feeling she had forgiven my misdemeanours and accepted my apology. She felt warm towards me, thank goodness. A few more waves washed over me; they were soft and peaceful, and I closed my eyes and once again I could hear the waterfall. Birds were singing and children were laughing and playing in the distance.

I lifted my head, opened my eyes, and looked round. It felt so peaceful, and I could see picturesque scenes before me.

Beside Marie-Anne, to her right, I could see my Bear who had joined us beside the tree. This tree seemed to be wider than I had first noticed. The Bear was sound asleep with a huge daisy on his head, and sporting a smaller daisy over each eye!

Oh goodness, how on earth am I supposed to remain silent with him trying to make me laugh? I do find it very hard sometimes! I shook my head and noticed a white horse, way off in the distance. It was so white it stood out easily against the countryside.

I lowered my head so I wouldn't get into any more trouble by giggling.

Marie-Anne appeared to be trying to say something, but I couldn't make out what it was. The waves washed over me again, and I wasn't sure if I was supposed to count them or make note of their vibrations. I did a quick re-cap in my head about what I'd seen and heard. There was the waterfall and stream, the banks with all the lovely bushes and plants, the plateau above the waterfall with trees behind it, birds, children, Bear etc.

Oh no! I thought. I've just spoken! Thoughts in your head come out as speech up on the Astral Plane, I remembered.

"Five minutes," Margaret gave notice.

I was pleased I had been given such a peaceful meditation, and that I could understand now, how much unnecessary rushing about I have a tendency to do.

I made my way off to the green mist, after once again thanking Marie-Anne, Arthur and all my helpers for making my lovely experience possible.

"What came through?" Margaret inquired with a big grin.

I re-told the very pleasant experience.

"That's how you should feel, calm and relaxed after a meditation," Margaret told me.

I realised that sometimes my meditations left me feeling exhausted.

When I told her about the children, she was surprised.

"You shouldn't have heard them", she said. She was observing us as she normally did. Apparently Saul, who is Margaret's Guide, had given her the ok to give the children chocolate as a gift. You can give gifts like that up there, she explained. How lovely. Anyway, he didn't think I would be able to hear them, but there you go!

Margaret had waited to see me settle down with Marie-Anne, then popped off to check up on Tom, and when she returned, the children were playing in the tree, very near to where I was, eating their chocolate. She had told them to be quiet so as not to distract me, and the weird thing was, that when I first thought I was hearing the children, I got a feeling there was someone telling them to 'shhh'!

When I described the white horse, she was shocked. Saul had told her she had caused havoc tonight, because the last time she was there she let the children ride on the unicorn, and they had him changing to their favourite colours, a bit like a traffic lights. She had told the children that the next time she visited the Astral Plane, she would let them have another ride.

"I'm glad I'm not the only one who gets told off!" I jokingly said to her, and then we both had a good laugh.

"Did you see a red rose?" Margaret asked

"No," I said, and then Margaret started to laugh.

"You must have spoken," she said. "If you had done it correctly, Marie-Anne was to give you a red rose."

I told her what I had done, the check list in my mind of everything I had seen etc., and as I was telling Margaret this, in my mind's eye, I could see Marie-Anne waving a red rose to show me.

Yet another glide along the learning curve.

The Dream

Now I wasn't sure whether to include this next piece in my journal, as it was a dream, but Margaret reassured me you can be 'sleep-taught' by Spirit, so I thought this might be a piece of a jigsaw puzzle needed later on; you can never be sure.

This dream has particularly stood out and remained in my thoughts for a while, so I decided to include it here.

Tom and I had been watching a programme called 'The Secret Millionaire', which focuses around wealthy people going 'undercover' as ordinary working people, and taking jobs with charities or alongside volunteers who work hard for causes in their communities. No one knows of his or her wealth. Eventually, the person of wealth decides how to distribute certain amounts of their money amongst these particular causes. It's heart-warming, and captures the essence of what I would eventually like to do.

The dream that night started with a face that appeared, and with the words:

"He holds the key."

Now this gentleman appeared to me as an older gentleman, with very distinctive features. He had mousey brown, thinning hair, combed over to one side and very thin on the top. He had big circles or 'bags' under his steely blue-grey eyes. His oval shaped face didn't look too happy, almost stern. His lips were thin, his nose long, and he was shown to me as tall, with wide shoulders, possibly with a bit of a stoop, an older version of Phil Tuffnell!

For some reason, his face seemed to be matched to an elderly gentleman I used to know years ago, when I worked at West End Dairy. That gentleman worked for an accountancy firm opposite our premises, and he was very similar in looks.

He never smiled and gave the impression that life was on a serious level for him, so back then I decided to see if I could make him smile. I did a bit of washing up and waitressing, so I thought I would make it my mission to get him to crack a smile. Over the weeks, and every time I handed him his lunch, I gave him the biggest smile I could, to see if I could get him to respond. It was hard work and I wondered if I would ever succeed, but eventually he smiled and always did whenever he saw me after that.

He was a hard nut to crack, so to speak, but one that I felt just had to be done! The face in the dream was that of this gentleman. What this meant I didn't know.

Then I saw an airplane that had ropey equipment, with a harness and a piece missing from it, possibly an aircraft from a foreign country. I wondered if this was anything to do with the business plan. Then in my dream, I was shown a massive warehouse with possessions, clothes, toys, you name it, it was all there, everything you would need to set up a home. It was like all the stuff inside had been donated. Some of it was packed in cardboard boxes and the rest just strewn everywhere. I thought it was a store for things waiting to be transported, maybe for a charity? I really didn't know.

Over the next couple of days, I racked my brains continually, attempting to piece together bits that I had dreamed, especially the name of the gentleman who had worked in the accountant's across the road. I felt it was important to remember his name, but I couldn't spit it out.

I was getting quite frustrated with myself and then eventually it came to me, his name was Mr Hope. And it all started to click into place.

'Have a little faith. Meet Mr Hope and help with little charities.'

Faith, Hope and Charity!

I had no idea what any of this meant, as I can see nothing on the horizon. It's intriguing and if nothing else, it's kept me entertained!

A Test

25ᵗʰ March 2009

"Tonight," Margaret explained, "you are to take the familiar route to the waterfall and then over to the tree. Meet Marie-Anne and she will take you to a mountain. You are to walk up a path and there will be a drop to one side. You are to observe everything and there are obstacles for you to overcome; there will be five of them.

Oh! Oops!" and she put her hand over her mouth, "I'm not supposed to tell you how many, oh well, too late!!" she laughed.

"You are to use what you like to get yourself up the path, but remember you are in Spirit. When you have got everything, there will be two Gatekeepers and a green wicker gate. If you have completed it all correctly the Gatekeepers will let you through. But if you have done it incorrectly you will have to go back and do it again."

Oh my! I thought. Given my recent track record, I did hope that this time I would get it right first time, though I did have my doubts, and that 'doing it again' was certainly a possibility.

I went up in the usual way, feeling Marie-Anne was with me before I rose up through the hatch. I followed Margaret's instructions to the waterfall, and met up with Marie-Anne by the tree of knowledge. We appeared to walk towards the bridge, and all of a sudden I felt myself walking up a steep, stony path, which I found difficult to walk on, and I tripped.

I noticed what looked like a cup and saucer to my right on the ground, and then I remembered that this had to be done right. There was no way I was heading off to anywhere without Marie-Anne glued to my side, and definitely not out of my sight. I would wait with her until she urged me forward. She was on the right side this time, I could see her grey habit and her white over-dress or apron beside me. I felt my hands getting hotter and hotter. Marie-Anne was holding my right hand and soon I felt her pulling me on, so I stepped forwards with her.

In front of me I could see a huge hedge, and asked her if we could sneak around the end by the mountainside, as to the left there was a sheer drop. At that edge I could see a blue staff with a light on the top, a bit like a warning beacon telling me to stay away.

I thought I caught a fleeting glimpse of an Angel, a translucent ice-white and blue colour, catching the light and then…. gone! We sneaked around the hedge to the right. I felt it was head height, and made of a type of privet. It looked as if it had been trimmed, and the end of it was beginning to get a bit thin.

Next there came a five-bar gate. Again, on the left hand side, was a blue staff with a light on the top. I told Marie-Anne of our favourite way of climbing a gate as youngsters: climbing up, bending over the top, grabbing the other side, and then swinging our legs over, and jumping down. I asked her if she was up for it and she agreed. We were over it in a blink of an eye.

The next obstacle was a brick wall, which was about six foot tall. The blue staff was positioned on the left again. To the right and above us, there seemed to be a bush on the mountaintop. There were no leaves that I could see, but coloured ribbons dangling down from it, almost like a rainbow, then on the top of the bush there seemed to be one big fairy light. I asked if it was possible to hop over the wall, just because we could, and then before I knew it, we were up and over, just like magic.

I couldn't believe my eyes! The next obstacle was a huge expanse of water, a massive wide, fast flowing river that dropped down over the edge like a waterfall, but I couldn't hear the water. It appeared deep and silent, and although I couldn't see the waterfall, I sensed it there. To the right, I observed a small rowing boat, and I can tell you, there was no way I was going to get in it. I would have to row faster than an outboard motor to reach the other side; the current was way too fast, and with that in mind, I tried racking my brain for an alternative method. I caught sight of the staff, on the left towards the drop off.

"Can we fly?" I asked Marie-Anne.

All at once we were soaring over the water. I could see and hear her skirts flapping in the breeze. We settled on the far bank and I could almost feel the coolness of the dark water against my skin, even though I hadn't touched it. Almost immediately, I caught sight of another river.

This time the river was made of molten magma. It was spitting its fiery embers into the air, and without a second thought, we knew we had to get ourselves away. Fast. I asked Marie-Anne again if we could fly over it, but this time as high as possible, so as not to burn ourselves.

As soon as we had cleared the area, we came to rest upon a grass bank with a green wicker gate. On both sides of the gate, were Gatekeepers.

The one on the left appeared bigger than the one on the right. They were both similarly dressed in what looked like battle dress. It was a dark green colour, with pockets on the chest and straps across the body. They seemed to be saying something and smiling, but I wasn't going to try and exit through the gate unless Marie-Anne pulled me through it. I stopped short.

"Can we go back and check that we've got it right? I'd rather check it again than have to come back and do it all again. Please?" I asked her. She agreed.

I felt myself going through it all again, though this time really quickly. It felt as if I was watching a high-speed movie of myself. At each obstacle, I checked it out for anything I may have missed or misinterpreted. Marie-Anne seemed to be ok with all this.

I waited at the gate and my hands grew hotter and hotter. Then we appeared to be through it and on the other side. Before me I could see a vast landscape of immense beauty. It reminded me of the stunning view of the Indian village from a past meditation, when it was viewed from the mountains.

It was then time to get back to the green mist and to the hatch. I thanked Marie-Anne and Arthur, my Roman soldier who is always present but not always 'visible'.

I felt that this had been a very demanding meditation and I didn't want to take anything for granted.

When I arrived back into the sitting room, Margaret and Tom had already left for the kitchen, for a cup of tea.

"Well?" Margaret asked with a grin

I relayed what I thought I had seen, and was met with a satisfied, "Yes and well done!"

I had passed the test! If I had not seen and done what I had, apparently, it would not be time for me to move on. Now I was ready, according to Margaret, to see my relatives and visit them where they live.

My mouth dropped open. Oh my goodness!

Apparently, on the meditation I had just completed, I was to see a sandal, which I mistook for a cup and saucer. Sometimes it's the colour that's required, if its form is different that's ok, depending on what is to be worked on for that particular meditation. In this case they were trying to distract me from the main objective, which was to deal with the obstacles. I had been expected, also, to see a temple, the Temple of Light, at the top of the mountain. Because I had been looking up, the light I had seen on the top of a bush was, in fact, the Temple of Light on the top of the mountain.

Margaret was pleased that her Staff was present, as it confirmed that she would be with us on every step we took. This meditation was to show us what we needed to continue on our path. Margaret also told me that she had witnessed my stumble on the path at the outset.

I just hoped I had already walked this path and it wasn't something that was going to happen on my earthly path. She was pleased that I had been presented with obstacles which needed focused thought to overcome.

The river and the molten larva were not what she was expecting at all, and she was delighted that neither Tom on his meditation, nor I on mine, had wanted to rush the gate at the end. We had both waited for our Guides to go through first.

Tom and I were really pleased with how our meditations had gone.

Phew! I was so glad I had passed the test, and couldn't wait to move forward learning more, with Margaret and Tom.

A Calming of my Mind

30th March 2009

WHEN TALKING TO TOM THE other day, I explained to him why I find it so hard to quieten my mind. On the table in front of us was a bottle of Barbeque sauce and I suddenly felt the need to explain a thing or two.

"What do you see?" I asked Tom, pointing to the bottle in front of him.

"Sauce," he said.

"What else?" I asked.

"Nothing," he replied. "Why, what do you see?"

I took a big breath, "Well… I see a bottle of barbecue sauce. It's brown, maybe an autumn colour, and on the label is a picture of the Houses of Parliament. That would be a lot of windows to clean. On the other side there are lots of ingredients that make up the sauce. I'm also wondering if there's any wheat in it, and I know for sure that there's vinegar in it, without even looking. The bottle is made of glass and I'm wondering how they made it and I'm thinking that if I was on a desert island it could come in handy. It's also possible to put this out for recycling. The lid is made of metal."

Tom quickly covered the bottle with a tea towel.

"Now what do you see?" he grinned.

"I see a cotton tablecloth that has white and blue checks and is very absorbent. It needs to be washed on 60°c."

"Okay, okay!" Tom yelled. "I can see what you mean. Your mind just doesn't stop."

"Yes, that's what I've been trying to tell you all along. When you tell me to quieten myself and not get so excited: it just won't! I can't be quiet. My mind goes forty to the dozen and it's only a fraction of what goes on in my mind that finds its way out of my mouth!"

"Oh, my gawd!" Tom muttered. "Now I understand."

We told this to Margaret when we next visited her and she understood completely!

"I'm a bit like you Grace," she said, and I felt relieved that she could see I really wasn't trying to be awkward. It was comforting, and I felt a calmness knowing that she understood.

Today, on my own, I thought I would go and have a chat with Marie-Anne. She was waiting for me up on the Astral Plane beside the tree. I had walked to the waterfall and caught sight of my blue crystal being charged in the cave.

Marie-Anne was pleased to see me, and we settled down in the glorious warm sunshine, it was a refreshing change from the cold winter we had been coping with *in real time*. It really was heaven up on the Astral Plane!!

Marie-Anne was trying to say something to me, but I couldn't hear. I was feeling a wonderful vibration up and down my spine. It made me shudder and then glow warm all over. Then I felt a bit dizzy. I had felt this before, but only for a fleeting second or two, on a few occasions. This time it was lasting longer, and with the dizziness I also felt a strange sensation at the back of my head on the right hand side, just off centre.

It was odd, I could 'see' in my mind's eye a miniature lift-shaft forming, with a square base at the bottom. I suppose I could describe it as a tiny corridor with a door at the back. The whole space was actually the shape of a mirror image 'L'.

After a few minutes the dizziness was starting to subside and my head was becoming clear. The clearness felt like a bubble encasing the area around the mirror L shape, which was then filling with a gentle golden light from above.

I couldn't make it out so I asked Marie-Anne what was happening.

"It's to by-pass the 'busy bit' in your mind and to make it calm."

Oh my gawd! I thought. I've had a brain by-pass!

Maybe I'll get a bit more sense out of it now!

It felt great, and I couldn't believe what had just taken place. I thanked Marie-Anne very appreciatively and actually felt very different, quite serene.

Over the following week, I must say I did feel more at peace and really calm. Bless her!

The Pyramid

April 3ʳᵈ 2009

Around the Christmas period, for no particular reason, I had a feeling that I would like to own a blue crystal but a pyramid shape similar to the symbolic one I had previously been given from the' true' Marie-Anne some time ago. I had no idea where this notion had came from.

Tom and I scoured the shops just before Christmas, hoping to see just the thing, but the crystal shops that we enquired in had never set eyes on one. I was sure I would see one somewhere, but had no idea where or when this would be.

This particular week I visited a shop I know well that sells a wonderful assortment of crystals and treasures. I happened across **the** most perfect blue crystal pyramid. It was not completely blue, but had a lighter blue-grey seam sweeping through it on a couple of its sides. It was made of Lapis Lazuli and the gold flecks that glistened from it made the whole thing instantly attractive.

I'm not a particularly materialistic person, and don't often see things that I just have to have, but without even thinking, the words spilled from my mouth,

"Please put this back for me Tony, I will pop back and collect it at the end of the week." And before I knew it, I was handing him *my* pyramid.

It was such a strange experience. It was like my brain hadn't really been involved in the decision-making, only kicking in to make sense of the words that were spilling from my mouth, as Tony was taking the crystal from my hand. Well! I thought. Someone has decided I need this one! I was so thrilled to be able to go in and collect it at the end of the week, and hadn't felt quite as excited to be getting something in years. It brought back memories of my childhood and the feeling of excitement at being able to go to the shop and get my own sweets.

I thought it must have some significance, so when I got home I asked Marie-Anne if I might talk with her.

"Of course, my child," came the reply.

I held the pyramid, grounded myself, opened up and was just about to go up on the Astral Plane when I could see my Bear in a room, in my mind's eye.

It was the very same room with the low ceiling that I first saw him in, when I was doing my Thai treatment on a client.

He had the pyramid in his paw and appeared to be dancing like an Egyptian. He then wiggled his bottom as if he had a grass skirt on! He looked hilarious as he moved behind me, and wiggled up and down my back. It reminded me of the Jungle Book scene when Balloo the Bear was scratching his back up and down the tree. I started to giggle, and then I could hear Marie-Anne telling me that the pyramid was a form of protection, and because it is blue it is also a communicator.

I was then shown a friend of mine Mark, who is here in *real time,* he is short and stocky, and very strong and always reminds me of a koala. I could also see my dearest friend and 'second dad' Philip, who is on the Astral Plane. He was always like a huge, cuddly teddy to me, but reminded Tom of a fierce grizzly Bear you most certainly wanted to keep on the right side of.

Next I was shown Edna, a lovely friend of mine who is on our earth plane, and reminiscent of a mummy Bear. She was a beautiful sandy colour, soft, warm and smiling, but with teeth that can be used if they were needed. I seemed to be looking down on a big circle. I could see myself standing in the middle, and there must have been about forty people around me, some turned inwards of the circle and some outwards.

The Bears were placed at intervals all around the edge of the circle and at the top of the circle there were two people who appeared to be a light blue-grey colour, the same as the pyramid. This couple were quite close; they then moved inwards and stepped to each side of me.

"This is your circle of protection. You have many who hold you dear, and for one reason or another, wish to keep you safe. Most people have this."

These words left me feeling warm, safe and comfortable. I did think that it might be a great comfort to many people to know this 'circle of protection' exists for them, too, especially in times of need.

I thanked Marie-Anne and asked her the name of this power animal of mine, my Bear.

"Bobo," is what I think I picked up on and with that, he started dancing again.

"Thank you Bobo," I said, and opened my eyes. I was still holding the pyramid *in real time* and when I looked at the underside of it, it was completely covered in sweat from the energy and heat coming from my hand.

The Inheritance

April 4th 2009

S AT AT THE TABLE IN my kitchen and chatting to Edna, a lovely
friend of mine, the subject switched from what sort of week she'd
had, to a former employer of hers.

She had once worked as a housekeeper and cook for a wealthy
family, and many a tale could be told about the comings and goings
of the guests, albeit some of them famous, and stories of the day-to-
day antics of the family. Edna was seen as a solid foundation whom
would not be messed with. The children, as did guests and other
members of the family, knew exactly where they stood with her, in
no uncertain terms.

The head of the household was a military man who had an air
of honour and dignity. He was a former officer and also held in very
high regard in his community.

As time went on, the gentleman and his wife parted company
and the divorce was made fair. The gentleman passed away three
years ago, leaving a will in which he left the majority of his estate to

his son, who in time, he hoped, would honour tradition and pass on the family name.

The father confided many times in Edna as to what was happening in his household, and for many years he had relied on and trusted her immensely: she was one of the few around him who was not affected or influenced by money. A spade was a spade to Edna, whether you were titled or not.

All of a sudden, sitting there in my kitchen, I could hear a man's voice. It was a rich-toned, well-educated voice.

"Edna"...and again, "Edna"..."Edna," he called.

I had heard this man's voice before, when Edna and I had spoken regarding the family and the children. He had just said hello to her on that occasion.

Edna was chatting away to me, nineteen to the dozen, completely oblivious to this dear man's desperate attempts to catch her attention. I had no idea what she was nattering on about, as all I could hear was his voice. I looked away from her and tried my hardest to tune in.

"Shh...!" I said.

Edna gave me a look that crossed between indignation and surprise.

"He's here and he's talking to me again," I told her.

"Oh!" Edna exclaimed.

Edna had been saddened by this honourable gentleman's death. This, in fact, was what our conversation had been focused on, when his voice came through again today.

"Do not concern yourself with my death. That is water under the bridge. What concerns me is the boy. He is not getting what he is due."

I conveyed to Edna what I was being told as she could hear nothing.

"Tell me what I'm supposed to do," said Edna.

The gentleman carried on, "A lady solicitor or barrister will thoroughly work through the paperwork and get it sorted. She must be told of all the facts and where to start."

With this, I could see a window in a room with a huge old, dark wooden desk on which there was lots of paperwork. It seemed to be situated in a distinguished looking property, and there was a small, thin-framed lady whose face and hair I couldn't see. She was out of the picture but I picked up on the fact that she had the most dainty, lady-like hands and was dressed in a powder blue outfit. She wore a couple of modest rings on her fingers, not huge stones. I felt that one of the stones could have been an emerald, but I wasn't too sure.

I could see the gentleman in question. He stood in a room with a window similar to that of the solicitor's, and I got the feeling that this may have been his home. In front of him was a huge, highly polished table, and behind him to his left was a cabinet or cupboard.

I could see a fireplace with a mantelpiece that had a Bear and a lion standing on it. They could have been carved from marble, but I didn't think they were actually ornaments at all. A big mirror with a decorated frame adorned the chimneybreast.

I turned back to look at the gentleman.

He was smoking a cigarette. He was of average stature and his thinning, light brown hair was parted on one side.

I sensed that this man had something wrong with his neck, perhaps, and possibly had a scar running down it. His right foot gave him trouble and pain. And then I saw his fingers. I wasn't sure what was wrong with them, but I was being shown them for a reason.

His voice came through to me again

"Tell the boy to negotiate with the solicitor, a 'No win, No fee's agreement. She will then get it sorted and the bill will come out of the estate."

The instruction I had just received had come through as clear as a bell. I relayed this to Edna, and she went on to explain that his son lived very simply and hadn't received his inheritance.

I had a sense that the gentleman didn't want his life's work to be wasted, and then I could see a pair of hands with silver liquid being poured into them; it was just running through the fingers, which couldn't hold onto it.

The fortune was literally running away!

Edna was amazed, and sat there with a huge grin on her face and then confirmed what I had told her.

Apparently he had injured his neck in an accident, and had trouble with his right foot and his hands.

The house I had described was his family home. The reference to the Bear and lion on the mantelpiece, rendered Edna speechless because these had been present in the house.

I saw him in profile. He looked pleased to have finally got his message through, and Edna, sitting opposite me, appeared equally pleased to have received it.

After some time, we heard that the young man had eventually received his inheritance.

CELESTIAL HANDS

5ᵗʰ April 2009

TACKER, A LIFELONG FRIEND, HAD taken a huge interest in these meditations. We grew up together, and over the years had laughed and enjoyed discussing life's pathways, sometimes together, and sometimes doing our own thing, but always wishing each other well in whatever we did.

She is one of those special people who you can pick up the threads with, whether it's months or years since you last spoke. We can always just natter on like it was only yesterday we were last together. I do love those friends! They never make you beholden to them, and you love them so much more for it.

Tacker told me she had a 'feeling' that she, too, has someone special around her, as if someone is looking out for her. She felt this had been happening more and more since she had heard of my exploits. Tacker's 'feelings' became quite strong, and she began picking up on a gentleman with wild red hair. She appears to be very tuned in and picks up a great deal, but does not realise just how much. She doubts her abilities, I keep reassuring her.

I spoke to Margaret to make sure it was ok to help Tacker, and she gave me instruction, and said that the most important thing to teach her was Protection.

Tacker and I went through the opening up process, and I gave her some homework as Tom and I had had. Her homework had been to find out and recognise the signals her Gatekeeper would give her when her protection was complete. It was revealed that the signal on completion would be her Gatekeeper touching her eye lashes.

It is a true pleasure to share such treasures with friends.

I needed further confirmation that I was passing on instructions accurately, so, having a quiet moment to myself, I decided to have a talk with Marie-Anne in meditation, on the Astral Plane. Once up there, and fully cleansed by the waterfall, I met her beside the tree. Marie-Anne introduced me to Tacker's Gatekeeper. I had seen him before. Tacker and I had been chatting the other day and I had seen him in my mind's eye, but I wanted to be sure that I had the right gentleman.

He did, indeed, have fiery red hair, as she had thought blue eyes and big freckles and was called Hamish. This is a name that Tacker, funnily enough, has always had a fascination for! She even had a cat called Hamish.

Marie-Anne explained that he had been at her side since birth. Some of his mannerisms are shared by Tacker: he is very funny and she is just like him.

So, dear reader, as I'm writing this I am actually having an *eureka!* moment.

A friend who I have been telling all about my meditations said- one day when I had been fooling around – that he could see similarities between the Bear's personality and my personality. ! Now things are starting to fall into place, and I am beginning to see similarities I have with Arthur and with Marie-Anne.

I do have quiet times when I don't require any company, these become more frequent if I need to concentrate more (so please, no-one take offence). I suppose this means that although you are yourself, it's possible you also have touches of your Guides and Gatekeepers about you, because sub-consciously, they do influence you.

Going back to Marie-Anne; she gave me a few more instructions for Tacker and then she appeared to be doing something for me. It came as a surprise, as I wasn't expecting any more. In my mind's eye I could see the room with the low ceiling that often appeared. This time I looked around, the only light that was coming in was from the trap door above my head. The room had no windows but one door at the far end. The room was full of desks, like a classroom. There were lots of people of all ages and races, all with a common interest that bound them together: to learn.

Then I realised that someone was teaching them; round the corner was a raised area with a teacher's desk positioned on top of it. Behind the desk, talking and smiling, stood,......... me! Marie-Anne was showing me what I am!

"You are a life teacher," she said.

I couldn't believe my eyes. It was very strange to see myself up on the platform, addressing others. There was some sort of spotlight shining down on me, and my hair and face were surrounded in a brilliant gold light. I looked radiant, bless them! Good job they didn't see me first thing in the morning! It was amazing, observing myself! If a little weird.

Marie-Anne then took me through the door at the back of the class. We entered a second room with exactly the same layout as the first one, but this time there were treatment beds, with clients, where the desks had been. I could see myself, this time doing healing and Reiki, everything quiet and serene. Others were also present, not many, about three or four, but it seemed that they were all apparently doing the same type of healing. The trapdoor was old and battered looking, as if it had been well used. The brilliant white light beamed down once again, just as it had done in the room before. Marie-Anne took me by the hand and led me through the door at the back of the room, into a third room, with a layout just as the previous two.

Desks filled this room too and I was sitting at a desk along with others. I could hear their voices and looked around at my surroundings. Around the corner, on the platform at the front, I could see Margaret and Sheryle. This time I was definitely the pupil and they were my teachers.

"Now is the time for you to concentrate", explained Marie-Anne. "It is very important or you will not move on", she nodded towards the fourth door at the far end of the room. This door, I felt for certain, I was not to go through today, and it seemed shut tight.

The trapdoor that I could see in this room looked like a new one, not battered and well worn like the ones in the previous rooms, but crisp and unmarked. I sensed that not many people had ventured this far. The only light present in the room was coming from this new trapdoor, giving a soft and gentle light.

Marie-Anne gestured towards Margaret and Sheryle, who were laughing and joking and making the learning fun. This was a lovely journey with the pair of them as our loving, knowledgeable teachers. I understood from Marie-Anne I was not to rush, but rather to enjoy, absorb, and to cherish it all.

Curiosity was getting the better of me, however, and I was desperate to see beyond the next door, not thinking for a single moment that this would actually be possible. The next moment, to my amazement, Marie-Anne beckoned me towards it and opened the door for me to have a peek.

My God! The light was so bright and intense that it was blinding. It felt so loving and caring, so incredibly beautiful that it made me cry.

There, I could see the most supremely graceful, celestial hands doing healing. The hands were the colour of ice, white and blue, just like the Angels I had seen. I could see souls with serene faces, wispy, delicate Spirits, floating around. The overwhelming love I felt made tears fall down my cheeks. I was in total awe of this breathtaking scene.

"This is what is to come," Marie-Anne told me.

A sudden thought dawned: I don't have to be....dead, to do this, do I?

"Of course not, child," I heard Marie-Anne answer.

Phew! That's ok then, just checking!

The door started to close, and I noticed how dark the room became, compared with that dazzling light behind the now shut door.

"Wow! That was incredible," I told Marie-Anne.

"This is the energy you will be working with if you move on," she explained.

So then I decided that slow and steady was the way to go, because there is no way I was going to miss any of this in my future.

Marie-Anne escorted me back to the gravel path and the green mist.

The journey today was a real eye-opener. It was absolutely fantastic, and one beyond my wildest dreams.

The Theatre

29th April 2009

Margaret had been on holiday and I had developed sciatica, over the last couple of weeks, so we hadn't had the chance to meet up. I was now signed off work and was wondering, with all the knowledge now surrounding us, if this pain in my backside had developed for a reason. It was obvious to me that the pain was not going to go away very quickly, so, was there something I should be doing?

Margaret had previously told me that your Guides would put you flat on your back if you don't take things slowly enough.

"Take it easy and rest up, as there is a huge amount of work to come", she said. The same had apparently happened to her, years ago. She hadn't been well on her holiday this time either, and was feeling exhausted.

Tom and I were supposed to be flying out on holiday in less than two weeks. I could not walk very far at that time, and was practically confined to barracks. The only position that I found slightly comfortable was lying flat. We were looking for some sort of miracle here, for sure.

Margaret arranged for us to visit her. I was so looking forward to seeing her again. It had been ages since our last visit and so much had happened. It was just like going to visit a dear friend as well as a teacher.

"Tonight, I have a lovely meditation for you and Tom," Margaret smiled. "You are to go up, meet your Guides, and they will take you to the theatre. For you, Grace, a black and white film to see, and you Tom, a play.

You are to look around and take in as much as possible," she explained.

"Ooooh! Can we have popcorn?" I giggled excitedly

"What are you like!" Margaret laughed. "You can have whatever you wish. Now, you will see three things that are important to your path.

Tonight, I will also let you decide when to come back down through the trap door." Margaret had that particular smile on her face, and I understood that this was another one of her gentle pushes to move us on.

We settled down in our usual seats, ready to rise to the challenge. Margaret opened us up, her familiar comforting voice guiding us through. I felt like a small child, waiting for a special treat; only it was us who were to make the treat happen.

Tom and I arrived up on the Astral Plane. Everything seemed so clear to me tonight. All my chakras had appeared really clear, like they had been cleaned and polished. My vision was as clear and crisp as it is in everyday life. I could see rabbits hopping around on the grass; a couple of deer grazing at the side of the riverbank; children playing in the fields. Birds and flowers were abundant. Even the trees and grass looked greener. We cleansed ourselves in sparkling, crystal-clear water.

I walked over to the tree and met Marie-Anne. She too, looked clearer than I had ever seen her before, dressed in her nun's habit and wearing a big smile.

"This way," she gestured, and we set off in the direction of the bridge, but we took the path just before it, off to the left towards the Elysian Fields. This path changed into a tiny tarmac road. We walked up a little way, then to the right of us I could see what looked like a small, empty, village car park, enclosed by a grassy bank which had bluebells and primroses growing wildly all over it. Ferns were unfurling and fresh leaves were beginning to sprout. It was like the beginning of Spring here, too!

We walked round a corner and an impressive building came into view, with six massive columns outside - three each side of a number of steps which led up to the entrance. Two huge, ornately carved doors providing further grandeur and elegance to the building.

Marie-Anne appeared very happy, with an air of excitement about her, and together we made our way up the steps.

"Can we dress up?" I asked, "Wear our best?"

I fancied myself in a long, white, floaty number. Marie-Anne appeared to be now wearing a white robe.

Well, I thought, it's not everyday that you get to go to the theatre!

Her beautiful long black hair was loose and flowing down her back, its silkiness catching the sun's rays and making it shine.

"What about tiaras?" I asked excitedly

She laughed, and then I could see a little dainty one placed in my hair. Well, I thought. I might as well go the whole hog!

As we approached the entrance to the theatre, the doors appeared to have been opened. I glanced back and saw the rolling landscape behind us. It looked lush and very green, the Elysian Fields stretching away for miles.

The tarmac area had no visible parking bays. Did they have cars, coaches or other modes of transport up here, I wondered? I've seen aeroplanes (where my Bear was the Trolley Dolly) but I think that's a bit excessive for the theatre!

As we entered the foyer in our finery, I noticed behind the reception desk on the back wall, an array of posters for forthcoming events. There were advertisements for different films that were going to be shown, with all the different viewing times. It was all very grand and a red carpet covered the floor we walked on.

I asked if we could have popcorn and there, sure enough, it appeared.

I wondered if we could sit upstairs. To our right was a grand staircase adorned with marble statues of (what I assumed were) Greek gods. They were armed with bows, arrows and harps, and all resembled 'heavenly beings'. We reached the top of the staircase and entered a majestic auditorium. Massive red velvet curtains framed the stage and were enhanced by rich, gold braid that decorated the pelmet. The seats, too, were upholstered in plush red velvet and looking around, I spied Tom and William sitting downstairs, over to my left. There didn't appear to be very many people here at the moment. I looked up at the ceiling which was covered in decorative artwork. The paintings reminded me of something along the lines of Michael Angelo's work. There were pictures of Angels and cherubs, all painted in the finest detail, surely true masterpieces!

I noticed that near the stage there was a woman sitting at a piano and looking ready for action.

It was then that I saw him, Bobo my Bear!

He was sat with us and had plonked himself on the right of Marie-Anne, cradling the biggest bargain-bucket of popcorn I had ever seen, the contents of which he was spilling absolutely everywhere. It was stuck all over his fur. It was on his ears, on his tummy, his face, all down his front, and I hate to think where else it had managed to lodge itself! His bucket was coloured red, white and blue and also sported stars and stripes. He stuffed his paw into the bucket and then was frantically trying to gobble the popcorn up that was sticking to his fur and everything else. The snuffles and snorts that were coming from his popcorn-clad face could only be described as sounds of pure enjoyment!

As Marie-Anne was to my right. I felt something touch my left cheek. I glanced round and picked up on some small children, shuffling excitedly in their seats beside me. I thought maybe they'd like some popcorn too, and their faces lit up at my suggestion. Even more squeals of delight came as cartons appeared in their laps, similar to those Marie-Anne and I had. The children and I all sat waiting in anticipation for the film to begin, scoffing our popcorn joyously. Marie-Anne was daintily eating her popcorn, putting one piece at a time in her mouth.

I saw a flash of blue in front of my eyes and thought it could be a pyramid but was not quite sure. Where did that come from?

The show started, with a black and white film which seemed to be Charlie Chaplin.

The piano joined in and was now in full swing. Charlie was ambling about, not taking much notice of anything then walked straight onto a garden rake, which banged him in the face. The old fashioned cars were in the clips too, and then appeared a delivery van.

"Is it a comedy Marie-Anne?" I asked.

She seemed to acknowledge my query by smiling, and then the picture changed to technicolour with Cowboys and Indians, the latter with spears, and one with long hair who seemed to be positioned in front of the camera with a small bundle- of- something at his left side. Others were joining him and I could see tepees and a huge buffalo. There were mountains in the background.

I became confused. Was I now at the Indian village? No, I could still hear the piano and we were all still at the theatre. Just checking!

The picture on the screen changed once more, this time to a whale swimming in the sea. It reminded me of the old Jacques Cousteau documentaries I used to love as a child. Then it changed back again, to black and white and Charlie Chaplin. The footage had the occasional lines running through it, as those old films did.

Fascinating.

The picture content changed yet again, and back to colour. This one featured scenes from Egypt, with pyramids, a Sphinx, and Tutankhamen.

I was spellbound and there was so much going on.

The picture changed one last time, to scenes from New York, Paris and London. This was all happening so quickly! Then it appeared to have concluded and I sensed it was our time to leave. We all stood up. I turned to the right and Marie-Anne stood aside. As she did so, I caught a glimpse of my Bobo waddling along between the seats with an empty bargain bucket, which was now stuck to his rear end…it wobbled from side to side and looked like he'd sat in it. Funnily enough it didn't appear crushed or bent but rather like it had suctioned itself on. There wasn't one piece of popcorn to be seen anywhere! He'd obviously enjoyed every last morsel of it. Off he waddled, with the occasional skip, down through the aisle. I started to giggle.

I felt that the green mist was calling, and now I could see it, so I thanked Marie-Anne, through my giggles, for a wonderful time and took myself back into Margaret's sitting room unable to contain the grin that had now stretched from ear to ear. It looked like Tom had arrived back at the same time.

"Come on then, tell me what you have been up to!" Margaret urged.

Just as I was about to answer, she turned to Tom and asked what the theatre looked like.

"It was big but I couldn't see it too well tonight," he answered, scratching his head.

"That's ok," Margaret reassured him.

She turned to me and I described the columns and the steps, with Tom agreeing. He described the door in greater detail than I remembered it as I hadn't taken that much notice of it, because Marie-

Anne and I, dressed in our finery, had been discussing popcorn. Margaret asked me to continue and laughed at our antics.

"I saw you all eating your popcorn, sitting in your box upstairs. I asked Saul to confirm it. (Saul is her Guide) What are you like?" she asked, in mock resignation.

As I continued describing my meditation, the smile started to drift from her face and was replaced with puzzlement. Oh no, I thought. I've seen that look enough times to know I've got it wrong. Was I running ahead again?

Marie-Anne was sat with me, or at least I thought she was.

My Bear definitely was present, that I know, but then he's also been with me when I've got it wrong before. Now Margaret's expression was one of utter confusion. As I finished reporting another part of the event she laughed once again at my Bear's antics.

She turned to Tom, he told of his experience and Margaret was pleased.

Her expression then turned again to puzzlement. Tom looked over at me and grinned. He also thought he had got his wrong, but she told him to carry on. When he had finished she looked at both of us and said, "Well I don't know what they're up to! Grace, you have seen things that Tom should have seen and picked up, and Tom, you have something meant for Grace. Now let's clear all of this confusion up. Grace, you were to see your Bear. That's fine. There's no confusion there. You should have picked up on my Staff, which is blue. You thought you saw a flash of blue, and interpreted it as a blue pyramid, but that's fine. Next, you should have seen an Angel that Tom saw. Tom, you should have seen your Indian Guide, and your Wolf and my Buffalo. Now Grace, when you saw the Indian, did he have a wolf beside him?" Margaret asked.

I wasn't sure, though I did see a bundle on his left side. There was so much going on, and at high speed. Margaret paused, then concluded that because Tom and I were so closely linked, we had picked up on each other's meditation.

"Well", I said to Margaret, "What about this - -Tom and I were talking earlier on today about our meditations, and we noted that Tom had not yet seen an Angel in any of his meditations. I thought he had, so do you think Spirit had given him the Angel just for the sake of showing him one?".

"It's quite possible, but anyway, you both got everything between you, so that's great! Now the things for your path with Spirit are your power animals, and your link with me. It would appear that as I am your teacher, it would make sense".

We were all really chuffed with that, and decided we deserved a cuppa, which we enjoyed with a giggle.

Tom and I had both seen the same décor in the theatre. Tom had picked up on more people present than I had. Maybe it was because we had our own viewing box. He saw a series of short plays, like mine were short films. He had Macbeth and a Christmas Nativity, also a play he couldn't identify. We were both chuckling over the bargain bucket of popcorn that my Bear had. Tom had seen the Bear and popcorn too.

It was during this visit that Tom and I thought we would chat to Margaret about how Tom's healing practice was progressing. He had been practicing his skills on me and it was going along nicely. He had picked up on many things that he was being shown.

My back had started to feel better for a while but had since started to feel uncomfortable again. Tom was certainly trying his best to help me. We combined our energies one evening, and I had felt amazing from that, but the pain in my leg persisted.

Margaret was interested in the Thai method of healing that I practice. I explained to her that I wished I could do this on myself, as I was sure it would sort out the pain in my back, but couldn't reach it, and Tom's hands 'wouldn't bend that way' as he put it, so I showed her how to position her fingers using Tom's spine.

I applied it to Margaret's spine she was impressed. As a nurse she is familiar with the conventional methods of pain relief; this was a little different to her.

Her shoulder had been giving her some trouble so I applied some of the Thai method to it; she was thrilled with the results, purely by paying a bit of attention to the different pressure points, her pain had eased.

After we had finished, Margaret thanked me and then apologised.

"I should be working on you!" she said.

So we arranged to meet the following week instead of waiting two weeks as usual, because Tom and I were supposed to be going away on holiday, my back permitting.

"Will we be going on holiday?" I asked Margaret, so she asked Saul.

"She will be skipping by then!" he replied

I had my fingers crossed that he was right. By now the evening was late and I was physically beginning to feel very uncomfortable.

Margaret said she felt guilty about having had treatment done on herself, but funny enough, all the time I was treating her, I had felt really comfortable doing it and the healing energy that was coming through was also having a healing effect on me! We decided that Margaret would work on my back next week, and she said it would be a pleasure to. Bless her.

We said our farewells and headed off home on a high, chatting nineteen to the dozen as we went.

What a fantastic, fabulous night!!

TEAMWORK

May 6th 2009

TONIGHT WE WERE OFF to see Margaret. This time it wasn't for meditation work but for healing. I was still experiencing considerable back pain and had been signed off work by my doctor. Physiotherapy was a good six to eight weeks of waiting, so Sheryle and Margaret said they would both like to do some work on my back. I was absolutely thrilled.

Margaret explained that if I was experiencing pain then I couldn't meditate properly and needed something done.

It was lovely to see Sheryle again. She was her usual bubbly self, with lots going on in her busy life.

Her business was at the point of going public and there was excitement in the air. There were numerous possible outcomes for her paint business to be thrown headlong into the public eye, and for it to become a resounding success. Health and Safety were showing an interest, so were British Rail and a British prison. The special glowing paint they had invented was certainly raising a few eyebrows and all it needed was for one firm order to set the ball rolling.

"Well go and get yourself comfy," Sheryle said to me.

I was so engrossed in listening to the progress being made from the paint that everything else had gone out of my mind, including the healing.

We went into Margaret's sitting room.

Sheryle had a good look at me and scan me with her hands while standing in front of her. She scanned down my spine, when she reached my hips I could feel this fuzzy energy all over, and what can only be described as a sort of pulling and tugging sensation around my hips.

"You had trouble giving birth (twenty three years ago). Your pelvis never went back correctly, and then seventeen years ago, something else damaged it further." Sheryle announced.

This detailed accuracy amazed me.

She continued, "You have a twisted and tilted pelvis and that's why you keep getting back problems. We are going to sort this out for you so that you never get these problems again," Sheryle informed me.

If Sheryle could do this for me, I would be eternally grateful to her.

My legs started to shake a little from the pain of standing and they made me lie down. Tom was at my feet, grounding the energy, Margaret was at my head and Sheryle doing her bit in the middle. It felt as if I had been plugged into the mains! The energy flowed through my hands and feet and I could feel 'tugs' all over my back and hips. Sheryle's hands weren't even touching me. As I work with Reiki energy I had felt this before, and needed no convincing that something was at work.

It was quite an experience for me, as having done plenty of healing treatments for other people I had only actually received healing for a pain when Tom had done some on me, but nothing on a scale like this.

Tom started to sweat and it was dripping on my feet. Margaret appeared to be having a hot flush and Sheryle was buzzing! It was fantastic and when they had finished, Sheryle said that it would take several sessions before it was completely healed. I stood up then had to immediately sit down, as I felt quite light headed. I was completely dazed. I was so very honoured that they had wanted to do something for me.

I had been in agony and now the pain had subsided to a large degree.

Tom told the others how and what he had felt during the healing, as wave after wave of energy was heating him up as it travelled down my legs. He grounded it all and did a wonderful job. Margaret explained that she had taken things off my shoulders and now they felt much lighter, and my hips, according to Sheryle, had had a huge blockage, so that energy had been unable to pass through them properly. Sheryle had done her best on that for this session.

I felt indebted to all of them for their help and was extremely grateful. They had worked incredibly well as a team and the energy that had flowed from Sheryle's hands was like a power surge, I was still buzzing from it all the next day. I felt it was a privilege to be part of this phenomenal group.

Obstacles

1ˢᵗ June, 2009

WE ARRIVED FOR ANOTHER LOVELY evening with Margaret; we knew it was going to be fantastic whatever we did. Summer had well and truly arrived and the drive down to Wishdal was an absolute delight. The evening sun made everywhere look beautiful and we acknowledged how privileged we were to live in such a special part of the world.

Margaret was delighted to see us and it's always so special for us to visit her. She told us she had a lovely meditation for us.

Tom was a bit worried he wasn't going to 'see' too well, as he was having trouble communicating with William. Margaret reassured him that this was only a passing phase, due to the fact he'd gone up a level and both he and William had to learn his new vibration. All would become clear in a while.

When you go up a level your body vibration changes to a finer level, it becomes lighter. You then have to grow used to it. I suppose you could say you have to learn to' tune in to it'. Much the same as you would find a different frequency on a radio, or television channel.

Tom was also feeling tired, which didn't help matters, but he was cheerful and eager to have a go.

Margaret explained that I was to go up to meet Marie-Anne, and that she would take me off on the path on the right of the oak tree, that leads to infinity. Margaret said there would be obstacles which would be part of our pathways. We were to observe everything.

We opened up and went up to the Astral Plane and cleansed ourselves in the waterfall. I did notice, in the cave behind the waterfall, that there was a white orb and a blue crystal. I went back to the tree and could see both William and Marie-Anne. I nodded to William and greeted Marie-Anne, and we moved off to the right, down the path, and I kept making sure that Marie-Anne's dress was still visible to me. I didn't want to march on ahead, and with Margaret's words in mind, kept looking around determined not to miss a trick.

All of a sudden, we seemed to be back at the obstacle course that we had done once before, only this time with a difference. The privet hedge was thick this time, and cut in the shape of a chicken at one end. It was quite big and the topiary actually looked pretty good. In front of me and to my left was the white orb that I'd seen in the cave; either that or it was one very similar. Behind that was a lamp to the right, and in front of the chicken, positioned on the floor, there appeared to be a pair of discarded sandals. I felt that they might have been left there for me to trip over, and was glad I'd spotted them.

I looked over at Marie-Anne. Was my mind playing tricks because I'd been given the word 'obstacles' from Margaret, and my mind strayed back to the ones I'd had before?

I'd had no chicken last time. Marie-Anne appeared to be gesturing and I didn't want to fluff it up this time. This had to be right. I asked if they were the same obstacles as before, and she was smiling at me. I took this to be a 'yes'.

I thought we'd fly above the hedge as we had done in the past, it seemed like a good method.

No sooner said, than done, over we went!

I was then faced with a stone wall made of light sandy coloured rectangle stones, very neatly made. Up and over we went, flying easily over the top again.

The next minute I was paddling in water, it was hard work. I had the feeling that there may be sharks in the water.

"Can we fly again?" I asked Marie-Anne. I wasn't too sure how many times it was acceptable for me to use the same method, and wasn't sure if I would be allowed to do it again. Before I had time to think, I had the sensation that I was flying but this time in a hot air balloon. We travelled over a huge expanse of water like the river in the previous meditation. I caught a glimpse of what I thought was molten larva, which vanished as soon as it had appeared. No where near the amount that I had seen last time.

The scenery then changed completely. We now stood in front of a pair of massive doors. My nose was so close that it almost touched them. I took a step back and asked Marie-Anne what I was supposed to do next.

"Knock, and very politely ask if it would be possible for us to enter," she replied.

I was thrilled that I heard and understood her completely.

I knocked and waited, looking over at a smiling Marie-Anne. The right hand door swung open and an elderly gentleman with a long white Beard and white robe said, "Yes?"

"Please may we be allowed to enter?" I asked him

He seemed to open both doors and gestured for us to enter.

In we walked to what appeared to be a large entrance hall with a marble floor, similar to the last grand residence. It was all very posh. I turned to Marie-Anne and whispered that it felt like I shouldn't really be here.

"Yes you should child," came her reply.

She led me over to what looked to be a minstrel gallery with a beautiful set of staircases leading up to a landing and bedrooms.

At this point I felt I needed to stop and just double check before climbing the stairs.

My attention had been diverted to Tom, back down in Margaret's sitting room. He had his usual slot on the sofa and was sitting about six feet away from me. His breathing had deepened, becoming so loud that I could hear him.

Oh no! I thought. I reckon he might be nodding off!

I tried to shake off what I could hear coming from Margaret's sitting room, and concentrate on what I was being shown on the Astral Plane. I was never going to do this if I started laughing, I told myself!

I turned my attention back to Marie-Anne, and we started to climb the stairs. Tom's breathing was becoming louder by the minute. It was like being back in church, when you get a fit of the giggles and try to stifle them.

Marie-Anne and I proceeded to the foot of the stairs.

Oh No! Tom was now on the verge of a rip-roaring snore!

Marie-Anne and I had finally reached the top of the stairs. She was showing me inside one of the bedrooms; the door was already open for me to walk in. I could see a big wooden window, with curtains that were tied back to reveal the most beautiful lawn outside. The room had big, dark wooden panels that looked like they may have been carved from oak, but I wasn't completely sure. To the right was a huge four-poster bed with thick carved legs, and in the bed there appeared to be some sort of lump.

No! It couldn't be....

But it was....

It was Tom, fast asleep! I could see his body heaving up and down and I prayed that he wouldn't snore out loud!

We turned quickly, and went out onto the balcony that linked to the other rooms. Marie-Anne took me to the edge that looked over the vast hall that we had just walked across.

I could now hear music playing and see people dancing. They wore old-fashioned clothes that could have been Victorian or even an earlier time. There was a swirl of beautiful colours as these lovely ladies danced with their partners. Their hooped skirts swayed and twirled in time to the music; it all looked beautiful and very grand. The music was quite old fashioned and sounded wonderful to my ears.

"This," said Marie-Anne "is how this house used to be, with lavish entertaining." It was a splendid sight and wonderful to see so many people enjoying themselves in this opulent place, then as soon as they had appeared, they were gone. They just kind of faded away.

The colours of the skirts had reminded me of wrapped sweets, as in a Quality Street tin.

"You have five minutes," Margaret said.

Tom was still resting his eyes!

I returned from the Astral Plane and into Margaret's sitting room. This meditation seemed to hold so much in it.

When we settled ourselves fully, I was relieved that I hadn't made a sound, as I'd been bursting to let out my laughter.

Margaret was interested in what we had seen, but alas for poor old Tom, he hadn't seen much. We had a laugh, and Margaret could see the funny side of my anticipation of Tom snoring loudly.

Dear Tom was still in a nice space, and Margaret laughed it off saying he had looked just like William his Guide.

After his 'rest', Tom said he thought he'd seen William on his horse and had felt he'd been with him on the horse too. After that, he thought he might have nodded off. Bless him; he works so hard.

Margaret asked me what I had seen, so I relayed my journey to her, mentioning that I was worried that I'd somehow relived an earlier meditation by mistake, because the obstacles that were present were the same, to a certain degree.

"No, you're right, it is your path, and you will see them again, but next time there may be obstacles you no longer see."

Thinking about it later on, I remembered I'd had a five-bar gate to get over before, and this time it wasn't there. The amount of larva I'd seen before had changed too, there was only a fleeting glance this time.

"The doors are what you must keep your eyes on, and that's what you must head for. That's you goal," Margaret said.

I wasn't sure in what context this grand residence was to mean to me, and didn't want to appear materialistic, so thought that perhaps it meant that one day I would be allowed to enter somewhere grand for one reason or another.

Margaret went on to explain that I was supposed to find a white flower, but I'd picked up on a white orb. It was the colour that mattered, not so much the object. I had done well because they had given me many distractions - the topiary chicken in the hedge; a lantern, which represents light; sandals to trip over.

"You are to be a teacher and an extremely good one. You are to notice the 'bright lights' that are to be taught. The distractions are to represent various 'distractions' that your pupils could/would throw up. You must learn to focus on the objectives of the lessons and not waiver from that course. You did very well."

I was really satisfied with the results I had achieved. When it all seemed to be a bit of a muddle, Margaret had made sense of it all.

While we were sorting things out, I felt I had to tell Margaret of a presence I had been feeling around me lately. Marie-Anne was here, but in addition I felt this stronger male energy around me, and wondered if she could pick up on what it was.

Margaret turned to Saul, her Guide to enquire, and was given a picture of a gentleman.

Margaret reported, "He is Sharamana, an Egyptian, and was on earth three hundred years after Christ. He was a craftsman, and he is your new

Guide!"

Now, **thats'** a teacher!- someone who can provide instant information.

Truly Remarkable Gifts

3rd June 2009

Margaret had excitedly informed me earlier this week, in a phone call, that Sheryle wished to speak with us. We were intrigued.

When we arrived at Margaret's we had a warm welcome, it was good to see them both, and we knew we were in for a treat of an evening.

"There are a few things we need to tell you," Margaret started out. "Peter, Sheryle's Guide told me to get pen and paper and has been talking about you. This is what he has said about you both."

We stared at the piece of paper that Margaret handed to us.

On the top of the paper dated 10th May 2009, (which to my recollection was a Sunday) this is what was written, verbatim:

"Grace and Tom.

Not by chance were they living in Salwayminster, as they had been communicating with Spirit for more years than they realised. Their future pathway is now before them. They have many avenues to explore so that they can realise and understand the true Spiritual gifts that are within them. We (Spirit) have seen what is within their hearts and their joy of reaching out and touching Spirit. They are a few amongst many who stand before Spirit and whose souls have the understandings of their destinies. Many shall come who will wish for their souls to shine as brightly as these two. Spirit shall see many souls there will be no hiding as to their true intentions before Spirit. Only those souls whose lights shine bright shall receive the true teachings and understandings of Spirit so that the lights of each soul shall shine bright and become One. It is with our gratitude of acceptance of their service. God bless you my children,

Peter.

They are as special in their own sphere as Sheryle and Margaret."

I could not grasp the enormity of all this at the time.

Margaret went on to explain. "Sheryle had been told of us three years ago. A special couple she was told. The man would be caring and talented, possibly an Earth healer, who possessed healing abilities and one who can see auras."

Wow! We had no idea what to say. It was magical.

Sheryle then moved on to what had happened to Margaret. She didn't mention what the woman of the couple would be like and I later wondered why, but at the time didn't even notice that she hadn't mentioned anything about her and I didn't think it was my place to ask. Maybe it wasn't very complementary and they felt it best not to say."

"Margaret had something fantastic happen to her last week," Sheryle explained. "She was given the key to a gift.

This gift is so special the last person to be made the holder of the key was eleven centuries ago, and she is to teach Tom and you.

-The Gift is the ability to lift the layers of time.-

When there is an event on Earth, it leaves a footprint, a bit like leaving a footprint in the snow, which can be seen if you tune into it. After a year passes, a layer of dust or snow forms on top of it so it becomes less visible, and after say forty years, the footprint is almost invisible. Margaret has been given the gift of lifting the layers," Sheryle explained.

"This can also apply to healing, and dealing with injuries too?" I asked in excitement.

"Yes," came Sheryle's reply.

"Back injuries like yours, which occurred twenty three years ago, can be helped. The layers of time can be lifted on that, too, and that is what we will be concentrating on tonight. We will start to lift those layers, so take your time and get yourself in a comfortable position on the floor."

Margaret explained that the new Guide was called Hikkamatis, and he had told her tonight that he would show Margaret how to lift ten layers. I was thrilled and didn't care if I was being used as a guinea pig. If it eliminated the pain, I'd stand on my head if need be! Margaret's lovely sitting room had huge sheepskin rugs on the floor so I chose the one that looked the fluffiest and most comfortable, and settled down. Sheryle was at my head, Tom at my feet, and this time Margaret was in the middle. Both Tom and Sheryle were to take away and ground the negative energy while Margaret worked her magic.

Well, I must say it was the weirdest feeling. It was as if I had waves washing over my arms and then down my legs. I could feel a pulsing in my back alternating with a lightness, which continued over and over. Tom was dripping sweat on my feet again, and Margaret was experiencing another hot flush.

"Oh! I'm getting hot!" Margaret exclaimed

"So am I!" both Sheryle and Tom chorused. Sheryle then moved opposite Margaret and the pair of them worked together on me. It was amazing! So many different sensations were flowing through my body, and then it felt like a wobble, and then another wobble in my back and down my legs

"That's all we can do for now," Sheryle announced.

"How did that feel?" Margaret asked.

I tried to explain, proceeding carefully, so I wouldn't miss anything out. The pain had changed, that was without question. Things felt very different. The heat, the waves, the different sensations, and all stages I was experiencing I had not felt before in this way. It was sensational.

It was now Tom's turn. He lay on the mat. I grounded, and Margaret and Sheryle both worked either side of him, like they had done with me earlier. I grounded the energy taking it down his legs; this bit I was more than familiar with.

Margaret and Sheryle worked for a while then turned to me and asked if I'd like a turn. Well, is the Pope Catholic?! I thought to myself. Too right I'd like a go!

I shot round to where Sheryle had stood and swapped places with her. I copied what Margaret was doing. The energy was strong, Sheryle was offering words of encouragement as I really didn't know what I was doing, just trying to copy Margaret and 'going with the flow'. I felt I should stay a while at the sacral area, even though Margaret had moved her hands up slightly to the lower lumber region on Tom's body. He was enjoying himself, feeling all the lovely sensations that were helping make his back better. He too had been suffering in the lumbar area.

We were all totally involved, excited, and chatting forty to the dozen. I was so proud and privileged to be part of the 'gang', and really felt we had bonded and become one special group. It was truly humbling for me. At conclusion, we continued chatting over another of Margaret's cups of tea, and then it was time to go.

Huge hugs were shared all round, and we thanked Sheryle and Margaret for the amazing healing we had received.

Over the next week, noticed my back had changed. It felt different and I hoped like mad it would improve. I was still listening for guidance and lying down when I needed to. I was also sleeping a lot, which Margaret said was good.

"It is Spirit's way of healing you quicker," she told me.

The message that Sheryle's Guide Peter had given to Margaret made little sense to me, so I decided to read it though again and again, dissecting the sentences, in order to uncover their true meaning.

Then the penny dropped…. I sat in floods of tears.

The true meaning of the message suddenly became obvious. It was almost too much for me to take in. Never before have I been given such a revelation of Their acknowledgement of my potential.

Chamberly Clairvoyance evening
with Sheryle Lewindon

8th June 2009

Once a year Sheryle and Margaret hold a clairvoyance evening at Chamberly town hall, and Sheryle shows what truly remarkable gifts she has by sharing one of them with us -- her clairvoyance.

It was about this time a year ago that we first met Sheryle and Margaret, and because of them so many things have happened in our lives, and so much has changed. It has been quite remarkable to say the least.

It's fantastic what following a hunch can do, like following the 'calling' of the chocolate box! You've got to follow it no matter what!

If it feels right, do it! That's all I can say.

We managed to gather family and friends who had shown an interest in what we were doing and who by now, were wishing to find out a bit more about their own lives. Some brave, some inquisitive, and some hoping not to be picked out at all but still wanting to experience and be part of the evening. We all finally arrived in Chamberly hall car park

Sheryle purposefully avoided meeting anyone from our group before the start of the evening, as it was possible for her to start picking up information on them before the event was underway. She asked me to pass on her apologises as she didn't want to come across as being rude. Our group understood completely.

We ventured inside and everyone took their seats. We chose to sit in the middle of the audience and left those who were feeling a little braver to sit in the front. Tom was introduced to the audience as living proof of what happens if Sheryle picks you out and you don't tell the truth.

"I delve deeper don't I?" she enquired of Tom, and people started to giggle.

Sheryle started off in her true style, bombarding people with information. It was coming thick and fast. There were so many messages from relations (with family tree history for verification). As the evening progressed, it seemed that everyone in our small group who wanted to be given a message, was lucky enough to have a relative or loved one come through for them.

It was truly amazing and so many stories were told. The evening stretched on and on and how she managed to be able to keep a clear head, and to continue to do what she did, I have no idea. It was impressive.

One lady, who had two disabled children, had an extremely helpful and practical message come through. A husband sent apologies to his beloved, long suffering widow, for his unreasonable behaviour.

Another message was sent from a grandparent to new parents, telling the new father to 'grow up'!

Then a truly remarkable message was given to a young mother who had suffered a miscarriage. She was told that she should not grieve for the baby she had lost as this baby had not been ready, and its body was not strong enough to be born yet. Sheryle told the woman that the soul she was grieving for would be returned to her at Christmas, in a new body.

"She will be 'Hollie', so don't worry, you have the most beautiful baby to come. She is waiting for you."

This was mind blowing! Everybody was hushed, and didn't dare breathe a word, and even the most hardened of hearts in the audience I'm sure had a lump in their throat.

I don't know to this day how Sheryle managed to deliver such a truly powerful message, containing such emotional impact, without bursting into tears.

This lady's reaction was a mixture of laughter and tears. All we could do was applaud loudly.

It was a truly heaven- sent evening with all the news it entailed. Everyone was in awe of what they had just witnessed.

After it all finished and people were drifting out of the room to go home, or to have a cup of tea in the kitchen, Sheryle asked Tom and me to join her and Margaret for a little healing; there was an elderly lady who was in need of some help.

It was Tom's first time healing apart from doing some on me. He did very well, and when we finished the lady looked a lot brighter and thanked us for our time.

It was wonderful for us to have been able to take our friends and family to such a special event, and to meet the lovely ladies, Margaret and Sheryle, who we are so fortunate to know.

Healing with Margaret's New Guide

18th June 2009

We arrived down at Margaret's where Sheryle was also in attendance. It was lovely to be seeing more of Sheryle as she was always very busy. Sheryle said that they had more for us to learn and use: apparently Hikkamatis had given Margaret more methods, involving different hand movements.

This time we practised on Sheryle, using the new methods they had to show us. Sheryle also wanted to experience how it felt as she hadn't received any healing last time.

Tom grounded and Margaret and I brought the energy in. It was lovely to help someone who obviously does so much for everyone else. Sheryle enjoyed the energy and said her back felt better.

There was so much to chat about and we nattered about the evening in Chamberly, and how everyone had enjoyed it. The messages that came through for our family and friends had fitted with so many things that were true. Sheryle was thrilled to hear the feedback.

The arrival of Margaret's new information about 'lifting the layers of time', was so exciting that we spent ages chatting about the different ways it could be applied to healing.

All too soon it was time to go. We couldn't believe how quickly the time had flown. We bid them farewell and made our way home, excited about all that had transpired.

An Important Lesson

8th July 2009

MARGARET WAS GOING ON HOLIDAY so we met for the next two weeks on the trot. Another treat!

I felt like a child having a storybook read to me, not being able to wait for what was to come.

Since starting with Margaret and Sheryle, the energy had been coming through stronger and stronger like never before.

Margaret said she was proud of me, although I wasn't doing the Spiritual healing yet, I was using the energy for the Reiki, and although it uses a slightly different system, it is still healing energy and this was flooding through and helping so much more with my Reiki.

Margaret settled in her chair; Tom on the sofa, vowing to stay awake this time. My chair in the corner was looking comfy, enticing me to join it! We were to go up on the Astral Plane, meet by the tree and then to go off in different directions. Tonight I was off down a leafy lane to the beach with Marie-Anne, where I was to observe the vibrations of animal, vegetable and mineral. Also, I would experience a feeling I was to remember.

Marie-Anne appeared younger this time, and we went to the left of the waterfall and off down the lovely leafy lane. I felt there were cobbles or rough stones underfoot. Beautiful trees and flowers adorned the hedgerows and I spied hedgehogs in the grass amongst the leaves and flowers. The lane all at once stopped, and there was the beach. It seemed too quick. I was really enjoying the walk and would have been happy to have carried on. The trees looked so lovely that I re-traced a few steps just to recapture the scene. Next we went down to the beach, once again too quickly to enjoy the surroundings.

To my left on the beach were Palm trees, and for a split second I wondered if I was wearing a bathing costume. To the right there were parasols, and what looked very much like my Bear, lying there with his shades on. Marie-Anne appeared to be showing me vegetation that was growing at the edge of the sand. Its vibration felt soft and had a fuzzy hum, but then I started to feel prickly, similar to the sensation I get when I feel the energy from my blue healing crystal.

I looked again. Marie-Anne was showing me something else, I could see a creamy colour, sparkly in places that caught the sun. She was showing me the surf. The image then changed and I thought I could see a dolphin.

My Bear appeared right in front of me, his huge form was laid out sunbathing. Maybe I was to feel his vibration? He did have a lovely hum! Then I felt a tugging at my heart chakra. It was a cold and extremely empty feeling. I felt that maybe this is what I would feel if Marie-Anne were no longer by my side. I felt sadness and then all of a sudden, Margaret's voice entered my thoughts.

"Five minutes," she said. Blimey, that had gone so quickly. I thanked Marie-Anne for her time and her help, and made my way over to the green mist which had appeared.

Margaret seemed thrilled to hear what we had seen. Tom went first, he visited the pyramids and I listened intently, secretly wishing my journey had taken me there. It was fascinating.

"What about yours Grace?" Margaret asked. I relayed to her what I had seen, only to be met with a look of disappointment on her face.

"Your bloomin' Bear is not supposed to do that. He was not supposed to be there. The dolphin you saw was meant to take you on a ride!" I was disappointed then, I never got round to telling Margaret about the cold feeling I'd had.

"Can I go back?" I asked
"Yes," she replied "You wanted to swim with dolphins when you went to Majorca."
I had no idea how Margaret had known that.
"Yes!" I uttered in disbelief.

I had been in agony with my back when we'd gone on our holiday. We'd already booked it so I thought I might as well be in a hot climate, resting my back on a nice beach in Majorca, than in England in my bedroom. It was a bit of an effort to get there but once we'd arrived, and after a few days there doing absolutely nothing, I managed to start getting myself about a bit.

During the second week we had watched a dolphin show which brought tears of joy to my face. I felt so humbled to be so close to such magnificent creatures. It was a case of beauty realised and very much appreciated. Such happiness was overwhelming me as they raced around the pool. They could jump to such astonishing heights and then show such gentleness around people who were swimming with them, and then suddenly tear off at great speeds again. It was breathtaking and wonderful to see.

Anyway, Margaret and Tom slipped off for a cuppa and I took myself back to the beach with Marie-Anne. There in the water I saw a dolphin. It came over to me and I eagerly grasped onto its fin. We dived up and down and I could feel the water on my face and the gasp for air as we came up to the surface. The next minute I felt I was being taken down again under the water to some beautiful corals, all colours of the rainbow, being made more beautiful by the sun shining down and streaming through the water, illuminating the scene even more. It was a wonderful sight to behold. Beside the coral was a huge, open, giant clam that was being lit up by the sunlight too, and inside sat a huge pearl about the size of a ping-pong ball. Around the curved edges of the clam were what looked like fine hairs, making the edge of it resemble an attractive cushion, soft and welcoming. It was quite magical.

We seemed to be swimming with more dolphins and I was feeling at one with them, gliding along as part of the pod.

I caught sight of a boat. At this point Spirit gave me another 'camera angle' on this experience. I could now see myself in the water with the dolphins, and then watch myself climbing out of the water and standing on a smooth, wooden, polished deck, dripping water everywhere as myself once more.

I didn't see anyone else but I sensed that there were others there.

I sensed it was time to go, so back into the water I went to re-join the dolphins and to return to the shore, where I was gently placed back onto the beach and re-united with Marie-Anne.

Wow!!! How fantastic was that! I couldn't wait to tell Margaret.

And when I did tell her, "Yes!" she said and I thought she was going to punch the air in triumph!

"You are just to slow down and smell the roses. If you go too fast you will miss it all."

Margaret told me that Sheryle had had a meditation where she rode a horse, with Peter her Guide. Apparently she charged along so fast she completely missed everything!

"You are going to teach. They don't want you to miss anything because your pupils will eventually be doing everything that you have done, and you must recognise when they have missed something.

I think your Bear is your inner child who plays and has fun. Now he must stand aside and not interfere. He is your power animal and purely for your protection," she explained.

The first time I saw him he was quiet and sensible, I told her.

"Yes. He will make a fantastic character in a children's storybook, as you have suggested, but not for now. Calm and tranquil is what I think you should feel," she added.

It wasn't quite like that, I muttered.

"During the meditation you should have felt similar to how you had felt in Majorca when you had seen the dolphins," Margaret continued. "You must remember that particular feeling, because that is how it should be for you now – calmer."

On reflection of Margaret's words, I felt that my Bear was possibly getting in the way of my progress now, and felt that although he was entertaining, it was now time for me to take on a more serious approach if I was to learn more. If I allowed my attention to be focused on him, I would miss my true lessons, and not only that, but people may not take me seriously when the time comes. It's ok to have a fun side, but everything in its rightful place. Even if Margaret did see me clad in a vibrant pink bikini with huge flowers on it and wearing a massive floppy sun hat.....

Consider my inner child/ Bear, told off!

I had a feeling I was going to be able to focus better for my clients, too, after this decision. I would be able to access more information given by Spirit. I just did what I was told. It was absolutely fantastic and I felt truly honoured to be part of it all. I was the telephone, and Spirit did the rest.

TACKER

9th July 2009

To tell you a little more about Tacker she has been a lifelong friend whose friendship I have always valued. She can't help but bring sunshine into your life, she never judges. She is always the same smiley, happy, open person and such a treasure. We grew up together, great friends at school through our teens, and onto when we each started our families. At this point we took different paths, and now we just picked up from where we had left off.

Tacker came for a Reiki treatment and became interested in the healing effects of the energy that I used. Her interest grew, so we started to meet up for regular natters over a cuppa, and she was interested in hearing about my meditations.

Tacker enjoyed every minute of the account I gave her, so it was an absolute thrill when she asked if it was possible for me to help her 'open up' and to feel the energy come through for herself. She has now met her Gatekeeper and Guide, and she has seen what a difference having a new angle on life can do.

When you have experienced something so special, it really is a lovely, satisfying feeling to be able to pass on the knowledge and techniques which form the foundations for such fantastic experiences, to a dear friend who appreciates what she is receiving and accepts it for what it is, simply 'out of this world'.

Tacker subsequently progressed to the following meditation.

I have included it here because it is also another part of my path. I wouldn't normally include other people's meditations, as I feel it is their story to tell not mine, but hopefully the reason for including it here will become clearer later in my writing.

Marie-Anne spoke with me on the Astral Plane as to what was to be given to her by Spirit and what instruction I was to give her. This is how it went:

Tacker made it up onto the Astral Plane under my instruction. (Phew!) She met her Guide by the tree and proceeded to the wood behind the waterfall where the green pool is located.

I could see her and her Guide clearly, and stood back to observe them, without being spotted.

She had gone into the water and appeared to be paddling, not swimming as I had hoped. Never mind, I thought, They probably have a slightly different agenda for her. She was to find some things of mine there, namely a white orb and a blue pyramid. She was to see deer, rabbits, fish and an Angel, if she looked hard enough.

I could see her sat on the Angel bench with her Guide, looking at something in her lap.

The next moment a beautiful white stag appeared beside me and nuzzled his nose over my shoulder, resting his head. I turned to touch him. His nose was velvety soft and I could see every hair on his muzzle. He was a brilliant white , as were his antlers. His hair felt slightly coarse as you would expect a stag to feel. It was wonderful to see this beautiful creature. Tom had seen him before, in the distance.

He was magnificent and I relished the pleasure of being able to touch him.

Turning back to see what Tacker was up to, I became aware of a gentleman stood in front of me, making it impossible to see her.

He was dressed in Egyptian finery: gold coloured robes inset with stones. His fitted coat fell straight from a mandarin collar. On his head he was wearing a tall, vertical headpiece, also a gold colour and inset with sparkling stones. His skin was a gorgeous olive hue and he had eyes that were framed with black eye-liner. Oh my!

"Hello!" I said (brightly?). "Are you Sharamana?" He appeared to nod and I felt as if Marie-Anne was giving me confirmation that it was so. He was a magnificent sight for any eyes, his presence was mesmerising, and it was fantastic to be in his presence. He appeared to be holding something which I leaned forward to scrutinize. It seemed to be a kind of bottle, and was made of lapis lazuli, the same precious stone that forms my pyramid crystal. The bottle wasn't particularly big, maybe measuring three inches or so. It was a light blue colour on the outside, with an oval shape on the inside that was a deeper blue, and enhanced with gold flecks.

I wondered what it would contain, and then I realised Sharamana was trying to give it to me. I was a little reluctant to accept it and decided I'd just have a slight peek. Were the contents inside a special potion of some sort? Then it dawned on me:

it contained incense, and with that thought came three of the biggest waves of energy which completely overwhelmed me. Was this a huge 'Yes'?

Marie-Anne appeared to be pleased, and I thanked Sharamana graciously for my gift. It was something else! I certainly hadn't envisioned anything like this happening, as it was my mate Tacker's meditation!

Now it was time for **me** to give **her** five minutes.

Sharamana seemed to have stepped aside and I could see her now. We made our way back to the green mist together and I felt thrilled to have seen her so clearly with her Guide, I thanked everyone for their time, guidance, patience and hard work for us both to have had such a pleasant time.

"Well?" I asked Tacker. (This was surely Margaret's line!)

"How was that? What did you see?" I asked with a massive grin on my face. She saw the right sort of trees; the orb, faintly; rabbits; and found a gold crown and necklace which she picked up to show her Guide. When glancing around she had seen the most beautiful Angel sitting on a rock under some overhanging trees, and she gave her the crown and necklace. The Angel put them on and Tacker felt that it was right to have re-united the owner with her possessions.

I was so pleased it went well, and very proud of Tacker; what she had seen and done was brilliant, and more or less what Marie -Anne had told me would happen. Good work! Tacker was thrilled to bits.

Later, when thinking of the incense, the penny dropped: incense......inner sense......sense of within. . . .

SHARAMANA

24th July 2009

MARIE-ANNE WAS CALLING SO IT was time for a chat. We weren't to see Margaret for a few weeks so I made myself comfy on my sofa and tuned in. Marie-Anne was not so clear at times these days and I was thinking it was because I had gone up another level, like Margaret and Sheryle had been expecting me to.

Marie-Anne was at the tree. The waterfall was refreshing, with rainbow colours sparkling through it. I turned to face the back of the cave and could feel the cool water running down my back. It was lovely.

Someone was standing in front of me.

Oh! It was Marie-Anne

"Ok, child" she smiled "This way."

She gestured towards the back of the cave and I followed on behind her, through the opening into the rear chamber. As I entered I could see a passageway to my left and what appeared to be a beautiful garden beyond it. Was it an orchard? I walked onwards and out into what did look like an orchard. I couldn't tell what trees were before me. Maybe they were olive trees, I wasn't sure.

We walked through long grass under the trees, the dapple shade was beautiful, a stone path with a bench came into view and we stopped at the bench where she sat quietly down. I could partly see a stream but things around me really weren't too clear today.

Two figures were walking towards us up the path, which seemed like a mountain pass with high rock on each side.

One gentleman was dressed as an Egyptian with a tall hat or headdress. Was it Sharamana? I couldn't see his face clearly on this occasion. The other gentleman I wasn't sure of either. He had thick blonde, wavy, shoulder-length hair, but I could see his face with vivid blue eyes, and he had a short Beard, almost like a 'Richard Branson with long hair'.

The Egyptian gentleman looked magnificent, unapproachably stern looking and professional, like he had a job to do and nothing was going to stop him. To me he looked as if he would walk through walls should he need to!

The other gent was casual and relaxed, with his robes swaying lightly in the breeze as he walked, smiling, towards us.

I turned to Marie-Anne to find out who they were, as I was a bit confused. Marie-Anne had previously said Sharamana was a carpenter and this elegant gentleman was certainly not dressed as a carpenter.

Marie-Anne continued talking to me.

"Sharamana wishes to give you the respect you deserve by wearing his finest clothes, to show you the standing he has, and how important he is to us both.

The other gentleman is Simon. He is to be found in the cave, gathering things that are needed."

Now I felt better. It's always a little confusing when you're not quite sure whom you have been talking to!

Sharamana seemed to be holding something on a tray. There were two things: first, a pyramid and the second item was a small box. He stood in front of me with his objects. The pyramid was blue coloured and the box was gold. The lid was open and inside was a shiny blue satin fabric. Resting on the satin was a heavy golden key. The key had what looked like rings on it or it could have been that the texture was raised and 'bubbly' like. It looked very old fashioned. Sharamana seemed to be lifting it out, and the bed that it had lain on appeared to consist of more keys. There was a total of five more smaller keys, all set down on their edge, resembling what I can only describe as a set of rings in a ring box showing only their upper parts. I felt Sharamana was gesturing towards me with the key so I took it and gently held it. It was beautiful and quite heavy, with red and green coloured stones inlaid. The other keys, I sensed, should only be looked at and admired and were not to be handled.

With this, I was now being shown a sign; a sign that looked like it could be made of brass or gold, I wasn't sure. It was almost like a cross, but instead of having a straight bit at the top it had an oval ring. I was not sure what it was although I knew I had seen it before.

I looked up at Sharamana standing in front of me, and a message was coming from Marie-Anne.

"Sharamana is giving you the key to your gift. As you can see, the main key also leads to a further five. These are *your* keys, my child. Learn the main one and the others will fall into place. Have fun, child and enjoy. Slowly, slowly, catchy monkey, smell the roses. Enjoy my child! Enjoy!"

"Thank you all so very much," I replied.

Sharamana bowed his head and stepped back and I did the same. I looked down and saw that the keys, the box and the pyramid were all in the palm of my hands.

Wow! oh my goodness!

I thanked them all very much for my gifts. I was quite overwhelmed. I made my way to the green mist and back down into our sitting room.

Because some of the things I was picking up weren't clear, I felt I needed to ask Tom to check with William his Guide, just to make sure.

Tom asked William if what I relayed to him was correct. William said it was, and that he thought that the keys I now held are keys that I have once held before, in an earlier time.

Tom was shown pyramids in the process of being built. He was then shown me stood with drawings, like some sort of architect… (Indiana Jones perhaps!) and I then, in my mind's eye, saw Tom within the picture as well.

Sometimes I can hear William, so I asked him what Tom was doing in these pictures.

Tom piped up "I am watching. "

I could see him in my mind's eye, stood on a patio or layer of flat stones, dressed in a white robe, just observing.

Tom then said that William was showing him, in his mind's eye, the top of the box with pictures on it.

Tom had been working at his computer, so we decided to research the pictures on the Internet and had a good look to see what we could uncover.

On top of the box was a picture of a cobra, a lion, the word 'Ramos' and two Anubis.

The next day, Marie-Anne decided to have a chat to me:

"Did you enjoy last night?" she queried.

"I did indeed," I said.

"Anubis was the protector of life and this is why Tom saw them on the box along with your signs. The keys inside are to be protected by these and must not fall into the wrong hands, for then they will become worthless and will not work."

Marie-Anne then told me to look at a picture that rests above the fireplace in my home. It has hung there for about six years, and is of Tutankhamen's gold mask with hieroglyphics written around it. I must admit, I'd never noticed the faint inscriptions before, but the sign that I had been shown that day was, in fact, now staring at me from the picture on the wall. It was being held by what looked like two Guides. They were kneeling on either side of a sarcophagus with a mummy lying inside.

Marie-Anne spoke to me once more: "Work only from the heart, my child, only from the heart.

Go in peace my child. Enjoy what the day's treasures bring you. With love my child." And Marie-Anne was gone.

I told Tom what Marie-Anne had relayed to me. Tom then told me that William his Guide was telling him that the figures are Guides or Gatekeepers of an important mortal.

We also discovered the sign I had been shown, is the sign of the Egyptian 'Ankh', their sign for life and protection. The sunrise is sometimes depicted with this sign in hieroglyphics, and many of their Gods were also portrayed carrying them.

Wow!

Messages and Guides

3rd August 2009

I WAS OFF AGAIN TO MARGARET'S home, this time on my own as Tom had to work late and he told me to go without him. Margaret decided to save our meditations for another evening so that she was not teaching us at different levels. It was easier for her, and for us, to keep to this arrangement. I was still happy to travel down to see her and it felt like ages since we'd had a chat over a cuppa or two.

We had had an offer put forward on our house since we'd put it on the market, and I felt in need of some reassurance from Margaret as to what was the right course of action. She had given us sound advice before, and had told us that we would be Guided. We didn't merely wish to move house, but to have a project that we could get our teeth into, so it wasn't going to be a straight move for us. I have always found living with lots of people around me rather restricting, so what I was looking for was to be able to fulfil a lifetime dream of mine to move into a log cabin, with a couple of acres of land, and to be able to live as eco friendly as we could. Not a small holding with pigs and chicken, wellies and mud, but more a place of peace and tranquillity, with a treatment room for beautiful alternative therapies.

At present we had no land, no log cabin and no planning permission, only an offer. Planning permission and land, we have discovered, was almost an impossible task to achieve.

Our plan was 'different' and many people had been very negative when we'd mentioned what we were looking to do, but Marie-Anne had seemed to be giving me the thumbs up.

"Its fine child, Spirit will provide," was what seemed to be coming through to me from her. Anyway, we had a start. One offer had been made, which we had accepted.

I asked Margaret if she would ask Saul for his guidance, and the answer came back telling us whatever we chose, stay or go, would be right.

"If you stay on the path of Spirit, Spirit will provide, and in a time of recession, you are in a golden position, "Margaret advised.

We had an offer. If it fell through then it was meant to be, we decided, and with that thought in our heads, we decided to 'go with the flow'.

We carried on nattering about the weeks' events. Margaret told me of her visit to a family wedding that delighted her. The interaction with her daughter was a thrill for her as always, and their conversation ended up focused on some make–up they had discovered. Margaret was eager to share it with me, it was some foundation that she had, and it apparently worked wonders for hiding her wrinkles!

I had been asked to take part in our town's fashion parade, to advertise local clothing and to help raise money for the local Mind Body and Spirit Centre. As a mature model of course! Believe me, I needed all the help I could get on this one! My facial lines, of course, are laughter lines!

Margaret introduced me to her wonder cream, which I eagerly plastered all over my face. "I can see a difference!" Margaret grinned, and although to me I couldn't see any difference whatsoever, her kind words gave me a glimmer of hope. I remained optimistic!

We chatted for a few more minutes when all of a sudden my face started to feel like it was burning. The idea of keeping my crow's feet, all of a sudden seemed more appealing.

"Oh! Margaret! Don't get me any of that cream, it's burning my face!"

"No it's not," Margaret laughed. "There's someone here. Sit down and open up. Take some deep breaths." She jumped down from her stool and dimmed the lights. "Ask Marie-Anne to help you and ask her who is here."

I tried to tune in but it was hard from a cold start, so to speak, and with flushed cheeks! Breathing deeply and trying hard to concentrate, I slowly managed to hear Marie-Anne's voice come through.

"Bill," I declared.

"Yes, I know Bill's here, but who else is?" she asked

I could see two figures in my mind's eye, coming into view.

"Simon!" I said

"No, not Simon, who else?"

I could make out a second person, but not very clearly.

"Ask them to step closer," Margaret suggested.

"J....J....J...J...J...J. It's a 'J'....Judas!" I cried excitedly.

"No!" came the familiar reply.

"J...J...J...J..."I was stuck with the J and couldn't seem to get anything else out.

I tried again. "J...J....J....Joshua!" I spat. "That's it! It's Joshua." Marie-Anne seemed to be nodding.

"Very good," Margaret replied calmly.

My chest swelled with pride. That had been so difficult.

"Now ask him why he's here. Is he here to visit or is he my new Guide?" Margaret asked.

"Both," came the reply.

"Ask him why he has come," Margaret instructed.

They started to show me a black ball that was huge. It was like a big bowling ball, highly polished and jet black in colour. It looked very heavy. I relayed the information to Margaret.

"What's it for?" she enquired.

Straight away, without time to think about it, the answer was spilling from my mouth.

"For you to see into the darkness," I said.

"Is it like a crystal ball?" Margaret asked.

"Yes," I said. It did seem to be like that.

Then They were showing me a dry stonewall. (I relayed to Margaret what else was appearing to me in my mind's eye.) It appeared to be on farmland, then I could see a style and a signpost, but I couldn't make out any writing on it. Marie-Anne showed me what looked like a stone chimney or some sort of building. It was situated on a hill with a valley beyond it, like it could have been used for mining. At the bottom of the hill was a small valley with trees, and then just beyond the wall, I saw a beam of light.

"This is for the children, and what you have just done is described perfectly a burial site. Can you see Sheryle and me there?" Margaret asked. This is a project they were working on.

I looked around.

"No, only a huge beam of light," I reported.

"Now the ground is opening up into a massive hole and the beam of light is focused in the centre. It's coming directly down. Now I can see four souls, each like a thousand diamonds ascending slowly through the light," I said in awe.

It was a beautiful sight, and so bright it made me want to cry. I smiled at Margaret, thrilled at what I had been able to see and what I had been shown. Margaret smiled back at me.

"We were told we would find four children," she told me, a huge grin beaming across her face.

All I could do in reply was blow out very slowly. Wow! Now I felt better, getting all that information out. No! Actually, I was chuffed to bits, big time!

Margaret's voice interrupted my thoughts.

"Grace, you were right," she said. "In that case, it was also Simon who you saw. He gets things ready."

"Like dispatch?" I giggled.

She laughed. "Yes, I suppose it is a bit like that. Can you ask Simon how long this will be, before these things appear?"

"A few things have to be put into place first. Your time scale and our time scale are different," came Simon's reply.

"Yes, I know," sighed Margaret. "Can you ask Simon if he realises that these things have to be financed and that the money has to be found?"

I got the feeling that Simon realised, and I was shown pots of Sheryle's paint flying out of a door. I stifled the urge to laugh, as it looked very comical, just like a cartoon. One pot flying out of the door after another, and the impression I was given was that Sheryle's paint would, in fact, take off!

We both had a chuckle at the picture that had been portrayed, and Margaret was thrilled at the message she herself had been given. She asked me to thank each of the Guides one-by-one, and of course to thank Bill, her departed husband, for coming. Bill seemed to be mentioning something about another cup of tea and I did feel that on this particular occasion, I really did deserve it! I continued to thank everyone for their time and for showing us what I had seen.

We had another cuppa and I said my goodbyes to Margaret and made my way home, desperate to tell Tom what treasures we had discovered this evening. It was exciting.

TACKER'S INDIAN VILLAGE TRIP AND MY SURPRISE

17th August 2009

TOM WAS TO UNDERTAKE ANOTHER meditation for Tacker. He had done one for her a couple of weeks ago, and Marie-Anne had told me that he needed to do this one and not me, as it would boost his confidence.

I talked us through the opening up, and Tom carried on with the meditation from the path on the Astral Plane. Tom wasn't really quite sure what colour the chakras were, and Tacker said that she really enjoyed the way I opened up, so that was how it went. Tom was quite capable himself, but they both wanted me to come along too.

It was lovely to see Tacker's face in reaction to the things she picked up en route, and while they were well into their meditation, Marie-Anne pulled me to one side and took me to the tree.

She said she had something to show me, and at my feet I could make out the feet of an enormous tortoise, that I felt must have been well over a hundred years old. I started to laugh, because beside it was another animal. This second animal was a pure white hare with the biggest feet I had ever seen. He was sat on his bum, scratching his ear with one of those colossal feet! The hair seemed to be young, and of course capable of great speed.

"Yes," I said to Marie-Anne, the message I had got through was loud and clear! "I know, I've got to go more like the tortoise and less like the hare….. Brilliant!" She smiled at me.

For Tacker, her meditation this time was to take her back up the path, past the hatch, and over the bridge to the Indian village. Tom had thought it could be a bit too advanced for her but I thought she would be fine, and so off we all went. As before, I thought I was there to observe. As it turned out, the pair of them were just fine.

All of a sudden Marie-Anne or Swishcannon, I wasn't sure who, was taking me away from them to another tepee. I had been quite happy watching Tacker's meditation, but They obviously had a different agenda for me. The tepee they took me to was possibly the one that Tom had visited before, the one they used for the village gatherings because it was huge.

Sitting Bull appeared to be there. We acknowledged each other and I thought I might give him a blue crystal, like the one I own, and a red cherry quartz, by way of my gifts.

They were always so generous in giving me gifts, I felt it was high time I gave something back, but never really knew what to give before. I had a feeling he might like these gifts and indeed he seemed pleased.

He held my hands again as before, carrying out some sort of inspection to both sides, and then bowed his forehead down to touch them. I felt truly honoured, and bowed my head as a mark of respect to him. He then appeared to put a ball of fire into my hands. Its colour was bright orange and red, and it was about the size of a grapefruit.

Funnily enough, it didn't burn or feel hot at all. As I was looking at it, I noticed that on the other side of the ball it was made of ice!

I was holding a ball of fire and ice! How unusual!

I was in awe of what I could see and then an amazing message came through from Sitting Bull:

"Fire is to destroy disease and ice is to combat infection." That is what he seemed to be saying to me, and that's what I thought I felt he said, but just to make sure, I asked Marie-Anne for confirmation and she appeared to nod.

Well! What can I say?

I thanked Sitting Bull and felt deeply honoured. What a wonderful tool. It was fascinating and truly out of this world: fire and ice joined together.

I got the feeling that this was to help with the healing that I would be doing later on. It was awe inspiring to think that I had the most potent tools at my fingertips now; all I had to do was learn how to use them.

Tacker's meditation went very well and before we knew it, it was time to make our way down to the green mist. Both Tom and Tacker made it back before me, as I was still thanking everyone. We all had a great time. You just never know what you are going to be shown next! Each meditation is a rich experience and always a joy.

THAILAND

26th August 2009

"TONIGHT EACH OF YOU WILL have a totally separate meditation. There will be a different message for each of you. Your meditations have moved up a level and will now start to contain direct information for you. Grace, you are to see something that you will think is Spiritually beautiful," Margaret explained.

She informed Tom that he was to see something relevant to him. I was thrilled and as usual, up for the challenge. I just hoped I could grasp what Marie-Anne had for me.

We went up to the Astral Plane and to the waterfall, and then met our Guides over by the tree. Marie-Anne took me off over to the path that led to the Elysian Fields.

We seemed to be just walking along and enjoying what appeared to be a lovely summer's day. It was warm and the fields looked beautiful and green. At the back of one of the fields there appeared to be a hedge, and I could see my Bear picking berries and eating them. Yes,

I did say 'picking' them, with his paws as well! I quickly looked away before he caught sight of me, and I glanced at Marie-Anne. He had got me into so much trouble in the past, and I didn't like getting into trouble and getting it all wrong.

"Acknowledge your Bear," Marie-Anne instructed. "He is your power animal"

I looked back at him and he turned around and waved frantically like an excited child. A pang of guilt rang through me for my intention to ignore him. He did love me dearly. This was so very clear to see, and it was like ignoring a lovely loyal friend.

In a flash he was beside me, so I looked up at him and told him that on no accounts was he to misbehave; he had to be on his best behaviour at all times, to walk behind me and not get me into trouble, and only on these terms could he come along. He seemed to agree with this as he shuffled himself in line. It felt like I had a seven foot bodyguard walking on behind me! It did feel comforting; I hoped we were back on track again.

Marie-Anne gestured to my right. There appeared to be a white colour and then a flash of gold, and I could see a Buddha, a bit like the golden ones I saw in Thailand when I went on my trip a few years ago. It was seated, bathed in a beautiful white and golden light.

Next, I could see Doi-su-tep Temple which I had visited, situated high on a hillside above Chiang Mai, with its unmistakeable golden roofs. Its huge serpent steps form a beautiful entrance to a truly incredible place. It felt peaceful and was also full of magnificent golden treasures.

"This was built off the back of others," came a sharp comment, which stopped me in my tracks. I hadn't thought of it like that when I was in Thailand. I was shown the grass huts that we had seen in Koh Lanta, another part of Thailand that we had visited. The latter was in the Southern part, which was a lot poorer in places. Some of the inhabitants could choose between having either a light on, or the T.V; certainly not both.

"These are the true people," the message said. "People who are in power and like the position they have, and don't want to lose it, will not help you, especially if they feel threatened with losing the power they have. The true people will help you."

Then I saw an old lady who had been on the last ferry as we started our return journey to the UK. We had travelled in a minibus from Koh Lanta and then island- hopped by small ferries.

The ferries were big enough for about four to six cars. For both journeys we had travelled in the dark, which was probably a blessing, as I couldn't see how deep the water was. The light was starting to break and things were now becoming easier to see.

This elderly lady was sat on the side of the ferry, alone and silent. I noticed she had only a couple of teeth, and her dress was well worn. The lines etched in her face told a story of a life of hardship; she touched my heart.

We had to go to Krabbi, Bangkok and then to Heathrow, and I still had some Bart in my purse (Thai currency) totalling about a fiver.

I was only going to shove it in a drawer once I got home. Something told me to gather it up in my hand. Then it was announced we could stretch our legs and have a walk around our minibus (on the ferry) as long as we didn't stray too near the edge.

Dawn was starting to break, and as I left the bus I could see that the light was beginning to reveal the outlines of the next island. It felt like we were crossing a river, not open water, because the islands were close together.

We chatted and the eight of us continued to enjoy each other's company. It had been a lovely trip. My companions were seasoned travellers and had many a fantastic tale to tell.

After about ten minutes it was announced we were to get back onto the bus. As we formed an orderly line, I was to pass the elderly lady, and in my mind's eye, I was being shown myself taking her hand which she would not mind, smiling, and placing the money in it and then closing it quickly so as not to cause embarrassment.

As I approached it felt so natural, and the old lady smiled back as I touched her hand; she didn't mind at all. I quickly placed the money in her hand and closed it tightly. The queue kept on moving and I caught only a glimpse of her reaction when we drove off the ferry. Bless her. She was waving her hanky to our minibus, but unable to see through the tinted glass at those inside. She had the biggest smile on her face. I felt both humbled and wealthy in the same instant.

I wasn't aware that Spirit had seen this and it was even more of a surprise to be reminded of it in this meditation. I had clean forgotten all about it.

"These are the true people with hearts," came my message.

I was then shown a re-run of a meditation I had already experienced, where I had been shown different paths and I had had to feel the vibration and choose the correct path. The meditation I had been shown was 'Which Pathway?' with one path that had Scot's pines and a beautiful loch; the other path I remember as being obscured by a bush, and because I couldn't see down it properly, I ended up choosing the more scenic path. I very soon found myself having to quickly re-trace my steps because the end of the path had led me to feeling a prickly vibration that just wasn't good.

The lesson on that occasion was 'All is not always as it seems'.

The message I had received from Marie-Anne appeared to be

"People in power will not necessarily help you," and that old adage, "All that glitters is not gold."

"5 minutes," Margaret warned.

Oh I do hope I have got this right and it's not my imagination, I thought to myself. I thanked Marie-Anne for all the information she had given me and made my way back down into the comfort of Margaret's sitting room.

Margaret asked Tom how he had done. It had been a very interesting event for Tom, he had picked up all the relevant information and some of it in great detail. There was mention of a dream we had of living in a log cabin in a tranquil setting and numerous other messages; he had so much to tell. It was lovely for him to have seen so much. He had gone up a level, which can make things a little fuzzy until you can 're-tune' so to speak. But now Tom was starting to repeat himself, and I was like an eager child, getting a bit fidgety having to wait until I could have my say. I knew I had to wait, hard though it was, and it seemed like ages.

Eventually Margaret turned to me. I started to relay what I had seen. Margaret's face adopted that' oh too familiar look' but I continued to rabbit on, hoping to see a flicker of recognition across her face that might match what she had written down in her notepad that Spirit had given her for me. I carried on, chatting forty to the dozen, convincing myself I had got it right, but having a sinking feeling that there was absolutely nothing written down about Thailand in her book and then I repeated the message 'What had been given was built off the backs of others' and it was then that her face changed.

Margaret beamed. I carried on, squeezing every bit of information out that I could, eager to keep the positive expression on her face, and to make sure that I missed nothing out, in case the bit I omitted was the only bit that I'd got right!

"That was fantastic Grace. Marie-Anne has worked incredibly hard for you today, and what she has done is nothing short of brilliance."

My chest swelled and I sat up straight to receive the praise. It was my moment of glory. It felt like I had gone from the bottom of the class to the top in a matter of seconds.

"Feet of clay," Margaret said. "They were showing you feet of clay. The people are not what they seem. They have feet of clay and shatter if they move. It's an illusion. What I had for you was that they were to show you beautiful white roses which were, in fact, made of clay and would shatter. What Marie-Anne has shown you is so, so much more, and is brilliant. Well done!"

I didn't see the roses, I confessed.

"I saw you looking at them," she insisted.

I remembered I had seen something white at the very beginning, before the golden Buddha.

"That was it," Margaret nodded.

I was so pleased, and both Tom and I had so much to tell each other on the way home. All of it positive!

The Biggest Surprise of All

10ᵗʰ September 2009

I SPOKE WITH MARGARET EARLIER THIS week, and explained I had been experiencing some headaches and found it very hard to tune in to hear Marie-Anne.

She suggested that I could have picked up some negative energy; if I had, it would need clearing. She then spoke with Sheryle who said she would come over to Margaret's, and if I visited she would kindly scan me over, to check.

"Spirit are attracted to the bright lights and you Grace, are a bright one!" Margaret explained.

Margaret and Sheryle scanned me and did indeed find some negative energy that needed clearing. As they worked on me, lifting off all sorts, my headache cleared, leaving me feeling light and energized. The headaches had started to make me feel sick so it was a relief to be rid of them.

"While you are here, let's get this Bear of yours sorted out," Margaret announced. "He should not behave in the manner that he does. Power animals do ***not*** do what your Bear does. His purpose is to Guide and protect you and give you power."

Sheryle popped outside to have a 'moment' as she calls it. I suspected she needed to have a private word with her Guide Peter. She soon reappeared with a smile.

Peter was sending through information at a rate of knots. Sheryle sat down on the edge of her seat and started speaking directly to me.

"Your Bear is ***very*** special. When you were annoyed with him and didn't want to speak to him, you nearly threw it all away. He has a ***very*** special gift.

He has the power of a ***Master of a Master of a Master***!

What he can do is gain the trust of children and this also encompasses 'the child within' the adult. This is so important for those children who have been so badly damaged that their trust in other human beings has been destroyed. The Bear can regain lost trust and connect with the souls of these children.

For example, they might be shown a farmer with a dog. They will befriend the dog and gradually associate the dog with the farmer. The trust will start to develop and grow, from trust in the dog, ending up with the trust in the farmer. The same goes for you and your Bear, but what he can do is even ***more fantastic***. The Bear can make the child ***so*** happy that the child's soul will open….

Your Bear has the ability to Read The Soul. Your Bear Has The Power and The Gift To Read The Soul!!!!

Now *you*, Grace, have to ask your Bear to teach you, and you will be shown how all this is accomplished. "

OMG!!! Wow! Tears started to appear. I couldn't quite take in the magnitude of what Sheryle had just told me. I thought I was going to get a telling off, now I was being told of the biggest surprise of all!!

"You will be taken to the stones," she said, "the sacred circle of stones where you will be invited to step into the circle, and you will be given the energy to enable you to do this. There will be Spirits with masks, half -human and half- animal faces. You must show the utmost respect even if your Bear starts mucking about, you must not laugh."

I had not seen Sheryle look so serious before. Peter was giving her so much information I had a job absorbing it all.

"The writings that you have and the idea about writing about the Bear for children's storybooks, is a really good idea," added Margaret.

"You must write the results of what your Bear has achieved," Sheryle continued.

"Wow! Wow! Wow! There must surely be a word other than 'Wow', but I've yet to find it and I can't think of anything else to say!" I gasped, squeaked, yelped all at once.

"None of us knew that; none of us knew what your Bear was like. **None of us knew!!!** None of the Guides knew the power he held. **Nobody** had any idea!" Sheryle sounded as taken aback as I was.

"He has been so very, very clever. He is, in fact, a shape shifter for the good, which means the loving tender playful essence of the Bear can inhabit other forms," Sheryle announced.

"It's fantastic," Margaret said, and she was absolutely thrilled.

"Have you managed to take all of this amazing information in?" Sheryle asked.

I nodded. I was dazed just thinking about what was to come.

"Have a chat to Marie-Anne and also to your Bear," Sheryle advised.

"Ask him if he will now teach you. You will be given this gift. This is your destiny. You have deserved it. It is truly a fabulous, fabulous gift."

I didn't know how to thank Sheryle and Margaret for leading me to all of this.

What did all this mean? How was my Bear going to teach me anything like this? When would I be ready? How long would this take? Where was I going to be using it? Who would I be helping? My mind was buzzing at all the angles this had just thrown up.

We had a cup of tea, which I'm sure never touched the sides; I didn't remember drinking it! Margaret and Sheryle were chatting, but for the life of me I couldn't remember what about!

When I returned home, I just didn't quite know how to tell Tom. I couldn't believe all of this was happening to me. When I did finally manage to give him all the information Sheryle had given me, Tom said both William, and Thainetua, turned round and **Bowed to my Bear**.

I tuned in and I saw this in my mind's eye, my Bear standing tall on his hind legs with his head held high, he acknowledged their respect with a gentle nod.

"They too had no idea he had such great importance, they were very, very impressed," Tom remarked.

For all his mucking about I had still loved him. It had all been a front, and now we all knew he was something so very, very special.

I felt so very highly honoured. Why me? I don't think that's something I'll ever know, but what I do know is that I have found the biggest treasure chest I could ever wish to have found. All I can say is the most heartfelt and enormous........

THANK YOU!

Epilogue

It is time for me to stop and take stock of the enormity of what is potentially at my fingertips. I need to think what effect this could have on my life and how it could change.

Could I cope with what is to come? Do I wish to walk forward and meet my destiny or stay as I am? This is huge.

I need to look back on what has been learned from Spirit, to take time to acknowledge what has to be learnt for the future, and to take the time to enjoy what is to come. I need to do this slowly and with inner calm, also, to reflect on the year spent with Margaret and Sheryle and their fantastic teachings.

I have travelled further Spiritually, in this last year, than in the forty five previous years of my life. I owe eternal gratitude to my Guides and Gatekeeper for their patience, guidance and unconditional love.

I believe the journey has only just begun...

I have found a friend in my Guide Marie-Anne, in fact, as you have seen, I have found many friends. What I needed to do was look within to locate them.

If this Someone is me, may I ask, could the next 'Someone' be you??!!

To You All,

I would like to say Thank You, for taking the time to share my journey. I hope you have enjoyed it and that it has lightened your heart and made you smile.

> What am I?
> What do I wish to be?
> **ALL** that I can be...
>
> Enjoy **YOUR** journey
> With love,
> Always, with love
> Grace.

Books that have inspired me on my journey and given different angles to explore include : The Celestine Prophecy and The Tenth Insight by James Redfield, The Writings of Florence Scovel Shinn, and the series of books Conversations with God by Neale Donald Walsch.

Music that has inspired a lovely space for me that you may like to listen to is: Bliss a hundred thousand Angels.

The Seven MainChakras

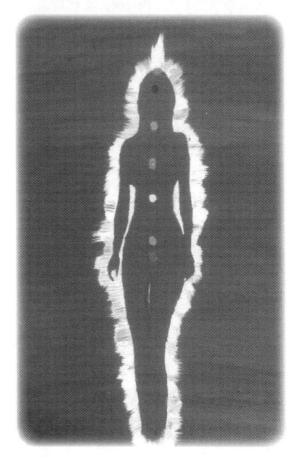

From bottom to top.

1. Base chakra. Red.
2. Sacral chakra. Orange.
3. Solar chakra. Yellow.
4. Heart chakra Green with a pink centre.
5. Throat chakra. Turquoise.
6. 3rd Eye chakra. Indigo.
7. Crown chakra. Violet.

GLOSSARY

Thai Massage is a traditional form of massage from Thailand that incorporates stretches, pressure points, massage, and energy lines, to cleanse the body of blockages, and so encourage the bodies natural healing process.

Reiki is a form of ancient healing originating in India that uses channelled healing energy to help those who seek help.

Chakras are the energy points of the body of which there are seven main ones. These points are used to give Reiki healing to the body.

The Astral Plane is a dimension that is used by Spirit to meet, converse, and teach us, while we are in meditation.

Gatekeeper is a sprit protector against negative energy.

Meditation is many different things to different people.